BOARD GAME
TO
BOARD ROOM

Board Game To Boardroom

MONOPOLY STRATEGIES TO NAVIGATING THE STOCK MARKET MAZE WITH CLARITY AND CONVICTION

MOHD AZHARUDDIN

© 2024 Mohd Azharuddin Khalid

All rights reserved. No part of this book may be reproduced, stored in a retrieval system, or transmitted in any form or by any means, electronic, mechanical, photocopying, recording, or otherwise, without the prior written permission of the publisher.

ISBN: 9798302913654

Published through Amazon Kindle Direct Publishing

The information in this book is provided for educational and informational purposes only. The author and publisher make no representations or warranties with respect to the accuracy or completeness of the contents of this book and specifically disclaim all warranties, including without limitation warranties of fitness for a particular purpose. The advice and strategies contained herein may not be suitable for your situation. The author shall not be held liable for any damages arising from the implementation of the material presented in this book.

First Edition

Dedication

To my dearest wife, Safina, for your love and support.
To my parents, Khalid and Hajira.
To my beloved sisters, Diana and Shameen.
To my nieces and nephews, Ayn, Ayaan, Ryan, Zayn.

CONTENTS

PREFACE	IX
CHAPTER ONE: BEYOND THE TICKER	1
CHAPTER TWO: SHARES OF DESTINY	17
CHAPTER THREE: BUSINESS BLUEPRINT	27
CHAPTER FOUR: MODEL OF EXCELLENCE	37
CHAPTER FIVE: ALIGNED AMBITIONS	49
CHAPTER SIX: TIMING PLAYBOOK	59
CHAPTER SEVEN: SAFETY NET STRATEGIES	67
CHAPTER EIGHT: MONEY MATTERS	75
CHAPTER NINE: MONOPOLY	87
CHAPTER TEN: RECLAIMING SUCCESS	95
INDEX	105

Preface

My journey into the world of investing in the stock market began after I completed my diploma in travel and tourism. During that time, I found myself unemployed and uncertain about the future. It was my brother-in-law, who worked with Morningstar, an investment research and management service company, in the Asian division, who introduced me to this fascination world of stock market which I have never paid attention to it before. He instructed me to file for my tax ID in India and catch a train to Mumbai to stay with him.

I started delving into the subject of the stock market with absolutely no prior knowledge. The concepts of buying and selling shares were foreign to me. However, just seeing stock charts and pictures of people working with multiple monitors displaying colorful charts captivated me. I was completely hooked and decided that this was how I wanted to do in my life by making money through the stock market.

Little did I know, it wasn't as easy as I initially thought. I bought an extra monitor, looked at charts, and engaged in impulsive buying and selling of stocks. I experimented with technical analysis - day trading, swing trading, position trading, momentum trading—you name it, I tried it which gave me a euphoria of being utterly alive. Unfortunately, I lost both time and money chasing the wrong ideas about making money in the stock market.

Preface

I have explored various technical analysis techniques, including patterns like the cup with handle, double bottom, and more. It's important to understand that many traders use these patterns hoping to make a quick profit. However, when thousands of people interpret the same pattern in one direction, and others take the opposite approach, the results may not be as expected. The stock market can often resemble a zero-sum game; for one person to profit from trading a stock, someone else has to incur a loss. Therefore, relying solely on technical patterns for quick gains is not always a reliable strategy.

As a retail investor, I realized the importance of building a strong foundation before making any investment decisions. The stock market is a complex ecosystem, dominated by institutions, pension funds, and large players who trade billions of dollars. These entities have the resources and expertise to navigate the market to their advantage. However, retail investors like myself can also generate wealth, even with a relatively small starting capital, by adopting the right mindset and strategies.

Building wealth in the stock market requires interpreting of financial statement and understanding business economics than making impulsive decision on information from media, analysts, and other sources which leads to ruin. We need to ensure that we are feeding ourselves with the right data and not making impulsive decisions based on misleading information, which can lead to our downfall. Retail investors often lack huge capital at the beginning, but we must accept the truth that our investments grow big from starting small. It's a simple truth that we

Preface

tend to complicate or fail to accept, expecting our investments to show a irrational gains in a year or two.

Consider the example of Warren Buffett, whose current net worth is estimated at a staggering $137 billion. Buffett's wealth grew exponentially later in life, primarily due to the power of compounding and his disciplined investment strategy. He became a billionaire at 56 and often emphasizes the importance of time in wealth creation. Remarkably, about 99% of his current net worth was accumulated after the age of 50. By age 30, Buffett's net worth was around $1 million, but his wealth surged to approximately $3.8 billion by 1989 and then to $30 billion by 1998. Buffett emphasizes patience in building wealth, famously stating, "The biggest thing about making money is time. You don't have to be particularly smart; you just have to be patient." His strategy focuses on long-term investments in companies with strong fundamentals, enabling him to ride out market fluctuations and benefit from compounding returns.

The important thing we need to understand is that behind every business that opens its doors, there are real people, like you and me performing well or poor in their work but least they work for their families to make a living which making it crucial that they don't lose the job. A decline in stock price doesn't necessarily mean that the company is not meeting the expectation, that it's laying off employees, or that its business model has completely failed. It's important not to make hasty decisions based on news, decline in revenues or temporary problem which can be fixed. Even if your investment doesn't show significant gains for a period of five years or more, it's essential to stick with it as long as your outlook on the business remains unchanged.

The stock market is designed to prompt impulsive actions, but having the opportunity to make decisions doesn't mean we must act immediately. Charlie Munger, Buffett's business partner, also emphasizes, "The big money is not in the buying and selling, but in the waiting." We need to wait for the right opportunity and allow our investments the time to work in our favor a principle we should strive to adhere.

Wealth generation should be slow and steady, guided by comprehensive financial planning that goes beyond just stock investments. While we are proficient at making stock investment decisions based on business economics or financial data, it's equally important to focus on our personal finances. Personal financial inconsistencies can hinder our wealth-building efforts. This doesn't mean we need millions of dollars to start working on our net worth. Instead, we should understand our net worth and planning our finances regardless of our circumstances. Investments begins within us, orienting us towards a successful life. Even a 1% improvement compounds over the years, paving the way for a prosperous future.

The stock market, unlike many traditional business ventures, removes many barriers to entry. Starting a business often requires significant capital investment, navigating complex regulations, and dealing with operational challenges like staffing, logistics, and marketing. By contrast, investing in the stock market allows individuals to become part of thriving business models with much smaller initial investments. Investors can focus on their choice of industries and companies, aligning their

Preface

portfolios with their understanding, interests, and risk tolerance. This accessibility democratizes wealth-building opportunities, empowering individuals to share in the growth of businesses they believe in.

The journey taught me to view wealth as a gradual process. It's about aligning one's investments with personal values and long-term goals, rather than chasing fleeting trends. I realized the importance of balancing financial knowledge with emotional discipline, building a foundation that could withstand market volatility.

Investing isn't just about financial returns; it's about personal growth, responsibility, and the power to create a future that reflects your aspirations. With each passing year, I've grown not only in my understanding of the market but also in my appreciation for the patience, strategy, and humility that it demands. This journey, with all its challenges and triumphs, has reshaped how I view success not just in investing, but in life itself.

CHAPTER ONE

BEYOND THE TICKER

"There is no such thing as simple, Simple is hard."

-Martin Scorsese

Investing in stocks is a fundamental component of modern financial markets, and it can be incredibly lucrative for both businesses and investors. But what happens to the money when you invest in stocks? When a business decides to go public and list its shares on a stock exchange, it starts with an Initial Public Offering (IPO). During an IPO, a company offers its shares to the public for the first time. The primary purpose of an IPO is to raise capital. When investors purchase shares at the IPO, the company directly receives this money, which can be used for various purposes, such as funding growth, expansion, and new projects. This initial influx of capital provides the company with the necessary funds without incurring debt, which can be particularly beneficial for businesses with strong growth prospects.

Warren Buffett, emphasizes the importance of understanding the companies you invest in. He often highlights the need for businesses to use their IPO proceeds wisely to create long-

Term` value for shareholders. For Buffett, investing is not just about buying shares; it is about owning a piece of a business that will grow over time. This principle is fundamental when considering IPOs, where the initial capital raised should be a catalyst for sustainable growth.

Once the IPO is complete, the company no longer receives money from the trading of its shares in the secondary market. After the IPO, the money exchanged in stock market transactions goes to the shareholders trading the stock. However, the company can still benefit indirectly from the price fluctuations of its shares. For example, if the current trading price of the company's shares rises, this increase in stock value can be highly advantageous.

Understanding the stock market's structure is fundamental to becoming a successful investor. When we purchase shares in a company, it's crucial to recognize what we're actually acquiring. Contrary to common misconceptions, the money spent on stocks doesn't go directly to the company unless it's an Initial Public Offering (IPO). Post-IPO, the value of the stock we pay is determined entirely by the secondary market dynamics driven by supply, demand, sentiment, and speculation rather than directly benefiting the underlying business.

The stock market often operates on principles that can appear irrational, creating valuations that might seem detached from a company's actual fundamentals. For instance, stellar businesses with solid growth potential can trade at sky-high valuations, while others with steady fundamentals might remain undervalued. This irrationality is where many retail investors stumble, as the market tempts them to solve what feels like an endless puzzle. The trick is to realize there is no missing piece; instead, the issue lies in not approaching the market with the right perspective.

The key to navigating this complexity lies in simplifying your approach and focusing on what truly matters. Warren Buffett's analogy of owning farmland offers a lesson. He asks, would you constantly check the value of your farmland every day or every hour? Likely not, because its intrinsic worth is in the crops it produces and its long-term potential. Similarly, the stock market rewards those who adopt a long-term perspective rather than acting to the noise of daily price fluctuations.

Investing becomes more straightforward when we filter out unnecessary distractions. A privately owned business, for example, can be evaluated based on its profitability, assets, and long-term growth potential without the chaos of daily price movements. Publicly traded companies, however, often come with added layers of complexity, as market sentiment can distort their perceived value.

Losses in the market can feel daunting, but they often arise when investors overcomplicate the process. The path to success lies in narrowing the focus to essentials and building a strategy based on disciplined research and realistic expectations. By resisting the urge to constantly monitor every fluctuation and instead concentrating on the broader picture, we can align our actions with our investment goals.

Simplicity is a strength, not a limitation. The market thrives on inducing doubt and overanalyzes, but by sticking to a straightforward plan rooted in sound principles, we can shield ourselves from the noise. As Buffett often reminds us, patience and clarity are invaluable. The challenge is not in finding the missing piece of a puzzle it's in realizing that the puzzle was never as complicated as it seemed.

A recent real-world example is Exxon Mobil Corporation, (XOM) acquisition of Pioneer. In 2024, ExxonMobil announced its plan to acquire Pioneer for $59.5 billion. ExxonMobil's high stock value played a crucial role in facilitating this acquisition. With its stock consistently valued at a high price, ExxonMobil was able to use its shares as currency to finance this significant acquisition without taking on additional debt. This strategic move allowed ExxonMobil to expand its access to the Midland and Permian Basins, more than doubling the company's footprint. By leveraging its outstanding shares, ExxonMobil capitalized on the increased stock value to expand its operations and secure growth opportunities. This demonstrates the power of a high stock price in enabling businesses to make strategic investments and acquisitions, maintaining financial flexibility and taking advantage of growth opportunities without incurring debt. Peter Lynch did emphasize the importance of companies using their stock as a currency for growth. He believed that companies that can leverage their stock value for strategic acquisitions are positioned for long-term success. This approach allows companies to grow without necessarily using cash, which can be beneficial for both the company and its shareholders.

Hewlett Packard Enterprise, (HPE) in its acquisition of Juniper Networks in 2024. HPE agreed to purchase Juniper Networks for $14 billion, a deal structured to leverage its high-performing stock. By using stock as part of the transaction, HPE was able to preserve its cash reserves, aligning its acquisition strategy with its long-term growth plans. This acquisition allowed HPE to significantly expand its networking business and offer advanced AI-driven and cloud-native solutions, marking a strategic push into cutting-edge

Square's, (SQ) acquisition of Afterpay in 2021. Square, a fintech leader, leveraged its high market valuation to execute an all-stock deal valued at $29 billion. The transaction involved issuing new square shares to Afterpay shareholders, effectively using its equity as a form of payment. This strategic move allowed Square to acquire Afterpay without taking on additional debt, expanding its presence in the "buy now, pay later" (BNPL) sector and strengthening its ecosystem of financial services for businesses and consumers. Furthermore, the acquisition was a synergistic fit, as it aligned with Square's mission of empowering individuals and businesses through innovative financial tools. Square's deal highlights the effectiveness of using stock as currency, especially when valuations are strong and align with strategic growth objectives. The transaction not only expanded Square's capabilities but also showcased the benefits of equity-based acquisitions for companies looking to make transformative moves without burdening their balance sheets.

Salesforce, Inc. (CRM) acquisition of Slack in 2021. Salesforce, a leading cloud-based CRM platform, acquired

Slack, a workplace communication tool, for $27.7 billion. In this deal, Salesforce utilized a combination of cash and its highly valued stock to fund the purchase. The structure of the deal involved Salesforce issuing shares to cover a significant portion of the acquisition cost, taking advantage of its robust stock performance to facilitate the transaction without entirely relying on cash or incurring significant debt. This acquisition allowed Salesforce to integrate Slack's collaboration technology into its broader ecosystem, enhancing its appeal in the enterprise software market. By leveraging its strong equity position, Salesforce preserved cash reserves while simultaneously expanding its strategic footprint. This approach highlighted how companies can capitalize on high equity valuations to pursue transformative deals, even in highly competitive markets. The strategic use of stock in such deals not only demonstrates financial ingenuity but also aligns the incentives of the acquired company's shareholders with the long-term success of the acquirer.

Understanding the concept of the stock market is crucial for gaining an edge when investing in stocks. By investing in stocks, you are essentially investing in the business itself. This perspective helps investors realize that they own a part of the business and have the same opportunities as the business does. For example, just as businesses can sell shares to acquire other companies or assets, investors can sell their shares to invest in other potential businesses within their portfolio. Additionally, dividends can provide a source of regular income.

Moreover, holding the businesses you invest in for the long-term allows you to succeed with the business through its ups and downs. By staying invested over the long haul, you can benefit from the overall growth and success of the business. Understanding the direction in which the business is moving and aligning it with your investment goals can significantly enhance your chances of success. John Bogle, the founder of The Vanguard Group, was a staunch advocate for long-term investing. He believed that holding investments for the long-term allows investors to benefit from the compounding returns and the growth of the businesses they own.

Market volatility is an inherent aspect of the stock market. Prices of stocks can fluctuate due to a variety of factors, including economic indicators, political events, and investor sentiment. Understanding and managing market volatility is essential for investors. Benjamin Graham, the father of value investing, advised investors to focus on the intrinsic value of stocks rather than short-term market fluctuations. He believed that in the long run, the market would reflect the true value of a company.

Studying historical market trends can provide valuable insights for investors. Over the past century, the stock market has experienced periods of significant growth as well as downturns. However, the overall long-term trend has been upward. This historical perspective reinforces the importance of long-term investing and patience. Charlie Munger, Warren Buffett's longtime business partner, advocates for learning from history to make informed investment decisions. Behavioral finance explores the psychological factors that influence investor behavior. Emotions such as fear and greed can drive irrational decisions, leading to market bubbles and crashes. Understanding these psychological influences can help investors make more rational and disciplined investment choices. Growth and value investing are deeply interconnected, often forming the backbone of successful investment strategies. When you invest in undervalued stocks with a clear perspective on future growth, you combine the principles of value and growth in a way that creates a powerful framework for identifying opportunities. Growth can come from a variety of sources: expanding market share, entering new industries, or acquiring businesses with untapped potential. Acquisitions can unlock significant profit potential if the acquired businesses are managed effectively. A deep understanding of the sector and industry in which a company operates provides the necessary context for assessing its growth potential. However, understanding a business is more than just knowing its products or financials it's about delving deeply into its operational model, competitive landscape, and long-term strategy.

The qualitative analysis of a business is often regarded as an art rather than a science. While quantitative metrics provide numbers that are easy to calculate and compare, the qualitative aspects require intuition, thorough research, and a nuanced understanding of the factors that drive a company's success. There is no secret formula or shortcut here. You need to understand the management team, their vision, the culture of the organization, and the broader market dynamics that influence the business. This comprehensive understanding forms the foundation of your conviction as an investor. When you truly understand a business, you gain the confidence to remain invested even during periods of volatility or uncertainty. This confidence is critical because markets are inherently cyclical, and all businesses encounter challenges at some point.

There are times when a business faces setbacks that lead to selloffs in its stock price. These moments test an investor's understanding and patience. If you've thoroughly analyzed the business and believe in its long-term potential, temporary setbacks become opportunities rather than threats. For example, if a well-managed company faces a dip in its stock price due to external factors like a market downturn or a short-term earnings miss, you can use this as an opportunity to buy more shares at a discounted price. The ability to capitalize on such situations separates successful investors from the rest. It requires a clear understanding of the difference between temporary problems and fundamental issues. Temporary setbacks often arise from external factors or one-off events, while fundamental problems usually indicate deeper issues within the company.

When you've done your homework and have a clear thesis for why a particular business is a good investment, you're better equipped to handle bad news or market fluctuations. For instance, if a business you've invested in encounters operational difficulties, your prior understanding of the company can help you evaluate the severity of the problem. By analyzing the situation and monitoring the management's response, you can decide whether to hold your position or take advantage of the lower price to increase your stake. Patience is critical in these situations, as solutions may take longer to materialize than initially expected. However, if the business fundamentals remain intact and the management team demonstrates a clear commitment to resolving issues, the long-term rewards can outweigh the short-term risks.

Understanding a business also involves recognizing its resilience in adverse conditions. Market downturns, economic recessions, and industry-specific challenges are inevitable, but businesses with solid foundations and adaptable management teams can weather these storms and emerge stronger. As an investor, you benefit from identifying such businesses and remaining patient. The real gains in investing come from holding onto high quality businesses over the long-term. The concept of compounding earning returns on both your initial investment and the returns that accumulate over time underscores the importance of patience.

However, it's important to acknowledge that even well-managed businesses face risks. A company's ability to recover from challenges often depends on the competence and ambition of its management team. If management is proactive and transparent in addressing problems, it signals that they are working to protect shareholder value. Conversely, a lack of communication or a history of poor decision-making can erode trust and damage a company's prospects. This is why evaluating management is a critical aspect of qualitative analysis. By understanding the track record and vision of the leadership team, you gain valuable insights into how the company is likely to navigate challenges and seize opportunities.

Investing in businesses with a growth and value perspective requires a disciplined approach to evaluating opportunities and risks. It's not enough to rely on quantitative metrics or market trends; you must also develop a deep understanding of the qualitative factors that drive a company's success. By focusing on the fundamentals, identifying temporary setbacks as opportunities, and maintaining a long-term perspective, you can build a portfolio that is resilient and positioned for sustainable growth. At its core, investing is about aligning your capital with businesses that you understand and believe in. When growth and value work together, they create a powerful foundation for achieving your investment goals.

Investing cannot be distilled into a purely numerical exercise. While quantitative analysis is essential in evaluating a company's financial health, it only scratches the surface of understanding a business. If investing were merely about reading financial statements, it would be a profession reserved for accountants. However, markets are far more nuanced, and successful investing goes beyond interpreting ratios and charts. Numbers can tell you where a company stands but rarely where it is headed.

The concept of conviction is what differentiates true investors from mere analysts. Conviction stems from a deep understanding of a business, its future prospects, and its industry landscape. This understanding is not something derived solely from spreadsheets but is cultivated through research, experience, and intuition. When an investor thoroughly understands a business, questions naturally arise about its growth potential, competitive advantages, market adaptability, and resilience during challenging times. These questions demand answers that quantitative metrics alone cannot provide.

To truly understand a business, an investor must dive deep into qualitative aspects. This involves analyzing the company's strategic vision, its management's ability to execute plans, the relevance of its products or services in the market, and the strength of its brand or intellectual property. The qualitative assessment allows an investor to gauge whether a business has a durable competitive edge or is merely riding a temporary wave of market trends. These insights must be reinforced by the numbers, as the qualitative must complement and align with the quantitative to form a cohesive investment thesis.

Conviction also plays a crucial role in navigating the volatility of markets. When an investor fully understands a business and believes in its long-term prospects, they are better equipped to weather market downturns. This is where the qualitative understanding becomes a shield against panic selling during periods of uncertainty. Confidence in the underlying business enables an investor to stay focused on the long-term, avoiding emotional reactions to short-term fluctuations.

Imagine discovering a stock that has escaped the attention of most analysts, is characterized by low trading volumes, and lacks the involvement of high-profile investors. These factors might lead some to hesitate, questioning whether such an overlooked opportunity could truly hold potential. However, the absence of these traditional indicators of popularity should not deter us from acting if our research and analysis strongly suggest that the stock is a hidden gem.

The essence of investing lies in the conviction built through our diligence and understanding. When our research uncovers a business with solid fundamentals, promising prospects, and a clear value proposition, it's an opportunity to trust our insights, even in the absence of external validation. The lack of widespread attention can often be an opportunity, allowing you to invest before the broader market catches on.

In the early stages of a stock's journey, it's common for high profile and institutions to stay on the sidelines, waiting for the market to validate the opportunity. However, as the company proves itself over time, delivering on its growth potential and demonstrating resilience, these influential investors often start taking notice. Their eventual involvement not only validates your thesis but also often acts as a catalyst, drawing further attention to the stock and driving its price higher.

For those who trust their analysis and take action early, this progression serves as both reassurance and reward. The emergence of notable investors in the stock reaffirms the merits of your conviction, acting as a metaphorical tap on the shoulder, acknowledging your foresight. It underscores the importance of independent thinking and the willingness to take calculated risks based on your findings, rather than relying solely on external endorsements or market sentiment.

The balance between qualitative and quantitative analysis is what transforms an investor from someone who simply buys and sells stocks into someone who builds wealth over time. The qualitative dimension adds depth to the numbers, while the quantitative provides a framework for evaluating the qualitative insights. Together, they create a robust strategy that not only identifies opportunities but also provides the conviction to seize them and the patience to let them grow.

The observer effect offers a powerful lesson in portfolio management, mirrored in the saying, "A watched pot never boils." This simple idea captures the essence of impatience: the more we focus on something, the slower it seems to progress. Have you ever wondered why this is the case? The pot doesn't boil any faster just because we're watching it; it reaches its boiling point at the right time, regardless of how much we stare at it. Similarly, in investing, constantly checking your portfolio doesn't speed up returns. Instead, it can distort your perception and create unnecessary anxiety, making it harder to stick to a long-term strategy.

The observer effect is a concept that transcends the boundaries of physics and psychology, having profound implications not only in science but also in investing. In its simplest form, the observer effect suggests that just the act of observing something can change its state or behavior. This phenomenon is well-known in quantum mechanics, where particles behave differently when observed. However, the same principle can be applied to human behavior, especially in the context of stock market investing.

Psychologically, this creates a sense of urgency where none exists. Investors who frequently check their portfolios may start to see patterns that aren't there, interpreting short-term declines as signs of impending disaster or thinking a slight increase is a trend. This can lead to a cycle of buying and selling, trying to time the market based on fleeting moments, rather than focusing on the long-term potential of the business. By over-monitoring, investors may be tempted to sell prematurely during a downturn, only to miss the eventual recovery.

In social science, the observer effect plays out in group dynamics and behavior. When individuals feel watched or scrutinized, their actions often change. This is comparable to the investor's reaction to constant market stimuli. Every news headline, every market report, or every market drop can seem like a reason to act, prompting a reactionary approach to investing. However, just as in social settings where over-watching can lead to behavior that doesn't reflect true intentions, over-monitoring your portfolio can lead to decisions that deviate from your initial investment strategy.

The concept also resonates with the idea that things take time to develop. Investments, like boiling water, need time to reach their full potential. Short-term volatility is normal, but the real growth of a company and the increase in the value of a stock comes with time. By stepping away from the obsession of checking prices constantly and allowing the process to unfold, investors can focus on the broader picture, just as a watched pot eventually boils without intervention.

Therefore, the observer effect teaches us that patience is essential in investing. A portfolio review once a year rather than daily or monthly checks allow for a clearer, more rational perspective. It is during these less frequent reviews that strategic changes can be made based on a deeper analysis of the market and the companies in which one is invested. Constant observation, in this case, interferes with the very process that allows long-term investments to thrive.

In essence, understanding the observer effect encourages investors to stop obsessing over the daily fluctuations and to trust the process. By not allowing frequent checks to affect decision making, investors can give their investments the time they need to grow. The real power of investing comes from the willingness to be patient, to observe less frequently, and to act only when truly necessary, based on a well thought out strategy rather than reactionary impulses. This, in turn, leads to a healthier relationship with the market and ultimately better outcomes.

Technology has revolutionized the investment landscape, providing investors with greater access to information, tools, and platforms. The advent of online brokerage accounts, robo advisors, and financial apps has democratized investing, making it more accessible to a broader audience.

Continuous education and staying informed are crucial for successful investing. Financial literacy and a solid understanding of market principles enable investors to make informed decisions and navigate the complexities of the stock market. Peter Lynch famously said, "Know what you own, and know why you own it." This highlights the importance of being well informed about your investments. Peter Lynch also advocated for investing in what you know, suggesting that investors should consider industries and companies they are familiar with.

Risk management is a vital aspect of investing. While taking risks is inherent in investing, managing those risks is crucial for long-term success. This involves setting clear investment goals and understanding your risk tolerance. Renowned investor Howard Marks emphasizes the importance of risk management, stating that "You can't predict. You can prepare." This highlights the need for a disciplined approach to investing, where preparation and risk management play key roles in achieving financial success.

CHAPTER TWO

SHARES OF DESTINY

"The stock market is designed to transfer money from the active to the patient."

-Warren Buffet

Shares outstanding are far from a simple concept. They serve as a crucial measure of a company's ownership structure, market valuation, and potential for growth. Understanding the dynamics of shares outstanding, how they are distributed, their implications on stock price movements, and the various factors that influence them can provide investors with an invaluable edge in navigating the complexities of the financial markets. These shares fall into two broad categories: restricted shares and unrestricted shares, both of which behave in markedly different ways and have different implications for the company, its shareholders, and the broader market.

To start, it's important to recognize that shares outstanding refer to all the shares a company has issued and is currently holding in circulation, including those held by insiders, institutional investors, and the general public. This figure can change over time as the company makes decisions about its capital structure by issuing new shares, conducting stock splits, or even buying back its own stock. Each of these actions can alter the balance between restricted and unrestricted shares and has direct consequences for stock liquidity, market volatility, and the overall value of the company. While the raw number of shares outstanding is important, it is the breakdown between restricted and unrestricted shares that truly gives investors insight into a company's stock dynamics and ownership structure.

Restricted shares are typically owned by company insiders such as executives, employees, or major stakeholders. These shares are not freely traded on the open market because they are subject to specific restrictions. For example, insiders may be prevented from selling these shares during a lock up period following an initial public offering (IPO), or they may be subject to vesting schedules that limit the ability to sell until certain performance targets or time periods have been met. These restrictions are designed to ensure that insiders remain committed to the company's long-term success and are not tempted to sell their shares at the first sign of a price increase, which could undermine investor confidence and cause unnecessary market volatility. Restricted shares are also a way to align the interests of executives and other insiders with the long-term health and profitability of the company. If executives are heavily invested in the company and cannot sell their shares immediately, they are more likely to make decisions that support sustainable growth, rather than focusing on short-term profits or stock price manipulation.

The presence of restricted shares in a company's stock structure often serves as a signal to the broader market that management has a strong vested interest in the company's success. This "skin in the game" mentality is reassuring to investors, particularly those who are looking for long-term value. However, it is important to note that insider ownership is not a foolproof indicator of a company's potential for success. Some companies with low insider ownership have still experienced remarkable growth and stock price appreciation, while others with high insider ownership have struggled to achieve consistent profitability or operational success. This means that while restricted shares can be an important factor to consider, they should not be viewed in isolation. It's critical for investors to perform a thorough evaluation of a company's financial health, competitive positioning, and market prospects before making any investment decisions.

Unrestricted shares, on the other hand, are those shares that are freely tradable in the open market. These shares belong to external investors—both institutional investors such as pension funds, hedge funds, and mutual funds, as well as retail investors who buy and sell stocks in the market. These unrestricted shares are what determine the free float of a company's stock. Free float refers to the portion of shares outstanding that are actively traded and not held by insiders or other locked up investors. The free float is important because it reflects the liquidity of the stock—the ease with which shares can be bought or sold without significantly impacting the stock price. A stock with a high free float tends to have lower volatility, as large transactions can occur without moving the price significantly. Conversely, a stock with a low free float may experience higher volatility because the supply of shares is more limited, and even relatively small changes in demand can lead to large price swings.

For investors, understanding the structure of restricted versus unrestricted shares is crucial. When there is a high proportion of restricted shares, the market may be less susceptible to large-scale selloffs, as insiders are unable to quickly liquidate their holdings. This can provide a sense of stability for long-term investors, as it suggests that the stock is less likely to be subject to short-term price manipulation or panic selling. On the flip side, a high proportion of unrestricted shares can indicate that the stock is more liquid and may experience higher trading volumes, but it could also make the stock more susceptible to market fluctuations driven by investor sentiment and external factors.

Take Old Dominion Freight Line, Inc. (ODFL) as an example. As of recent reports, ODFL had approximately 214 million outstanding shares. Out of these, around 23 million shares were restricted, meaning insiders held these shares and could not trade them freely on the open market. This represents about 11% of the total outstanding shares, signaling that the company's management and employees have a substantial financial interest in the company's performance. The remaining 168 million shares, or 78%, are held by institutional investors large entities such as mutual funds, pension funds, and hedge funds. The remaining 11% of shares, or 23 million, are considered the free float and are available for retail investors to buy and sell on the stock exchange. From this ownership breakdown, it is clear that ODFL is controlled by a combination of insiders and institutional investors, with only a small percentage of shares available to retail investors. This ownership structure can influence the liquidity of the stock and can provide valuable insights into the company's stability and growth potential.

While understanding the ownership structure of a company is vital, it is equally important to recognize how share issuance, stock buybacks, and dilution can affect shares outstanding and, consequently, the stock price. Share issuance is one of the primary ways that companies can raise capital. By issuing new shares, companies can access funds to finance expansion, pay off debt, or fund other capital projects. However, issuing additional shares increases the total number of shares outstanding, which can lead to dilution for existing shareholders. Dilution occurs when a company increases its share count without a corresponding increase in the company's value. As a result, each existing shareholder's stake in the company becomes smaller, and their shares are worth slightly less. While issuing shares can be a useful tool for companies to raise capital, investors must carefully evaluate the purpose of the issuance. If the capital raised is being used for profitable growth opportunities, such as expanding the company's operations or investing in new technologies, the issuance may ultimately lead to long-term value creation. However, if the funds are used to pay off debt or cover operating losses, the issuance could signal trouble for the company's future prospects and could negatively affect shareholder value.

Share repurchases, commonly known as stock buybacks, are a potent mechanism through which companies can deliver value to shareholders. By reducing the number of shares outstanding, share buybacks increase the ownership percentage of each remaining shareholder, often enhancing the value of their shares. However, this process is most effective when executed with precision and strategy. Companies that repurchase their shares when the stock price is trading below intrinsic value are not merely returning capital to shareholders; they are also signaling confidence in the company's future prospects and their own valuation analysis. This ensures that buybacks yield maximum benefit by effectively reallocating capital in a manner that supports long-term shareholder value.

On the flip side, issuing shares at times when the stock price is near or above its fair value can also be an effective strategy. When a company's shares are in high demand and trading at a premium, issuing new shares allows the company to raise capital without significantly diluting existing shareholders. This capital can then be deployed towards growth initiatives, acquisitions, or other value creating opportunities. The balance between repurchasing shares and issuing them requires management to have an acute understanding of the company's intrinsic value and market dynamics.

The critical aspect for investors to grasp is that these corporate actions buybacks and share issuances work over time and align with the broader goals of long-term wealth creation. Share repurchases should not be misconstrued as a short-term tactic to artificially inflate stock prices but rather as a reflection of prudent capital allocation. When executed at below intrinsic value levels, buybacks represent one of the most efficient uses of a company's cash reserves. Conversely, share issuances at overvalued levels enable companies to maximize the inflow of resources, mitigating potential dilution effects and positioning themselves for future growth. It is also worth addressing a common misconception among investors regarding share issuance. Many perceive share dilution as inherently negative, but this view is often shortsighted. Long-term investors, especially those who understand the strategic reasoning behind these actions, are well positioned to benefit. For instance, when shares are issued to fund acquisitions or expand business operations, the resulting growth can significantly outweigh the dilutive impact, ultimately creating net value for shareholders. Similarly, buybacks executed during opportune times provide an avenue for long-term investors to amplify their equity stake and reap compounding benefits. It is a long-term strategy that demands discipline, foresight, and a deep commitment to creating shareholder value.

Copart, Inc (CPRT) provides online auctions and vehicle remarketing services in the United States, Canada, the United Kingdom, Brazil, the Republic of Ireland, Germany, Finland, the United Arab Emirates, Oman, Bahrain, and Spain. has demonstrated a keen ability to utilize share issuance as a tool for enhancing shareholder value while maintaining a steady share price. By strategically raising capital through issuing shares, the company has been able to fund key business initiatives, such as expanding its global reach, improving technology, and acquiring assets that strengthen its market position. These actions, while initially leading to an increase in shares outstanding, have been aligned with long-term business goals that contribute to higher earnings potential and increased market share.

What sets Copart apart is its careful balance between capital raising and share price management. When the company issues shares, it does so with the intent of reinvesting in profitable ventures, which are expected to generate returns greater than the cost of capital. As a result, Copart's strategic use of share issuance has often been accompanied by initiatives that drive long-term growth and operational efficiency, which in turn help maintain or even increase its share price.

Moreover, Copart has consistently shown that its decisions to issue shares are not done to dilute value, but rather to fund initiatives that directly benefit shareholders. By ensuring that the funds raised are allocated towards growth strategies that enhance the company's competitive advantage and profitability, Copart has managed to uphold its reputation for delivering shareholder value while mitigating the risks typically associated with share dilution. This careful, measured approach to capital management demonstrates how share issuance can be a powerful tool in improving business economics without undermining stock price stability

Through a comprehensive understanding of shares outstanding, an investor can become better equipped to make informed decisions. Understanding the forces that drive stock valuation, market dynamics, and ownership structure enables investors to not only analyze the present state of a company but also to anticipate its future potential. This approach is essential for building a robust, long-term investment strategy. By remaining patient, diligent, and focused on the fundamentals, investors can identify opportunities ahead of the market and capitalize on undervalued stocks or emerging growth trends before they become widely recognized. With this knowledge, retail investors can confidently participate in the market, aligning their interests with those of the company's leadership and institutional investors, and ultimately contributing to their own financial success.

CHAPTER THREE

BUSINESS BLUEPRINT

"If you want to have a better chance of success in the stock market, you have to have a better understanding of the business."

-Philip Fisher

In the vast landscape of the stock market, with thousands of companies competing for attention, the challenge of selecting the right stocks can feel overwhelming. Successful investing requires more than just intuition or luck it demands a well thought out strategy grounded in research, analysis, and an understanding of market dynamics. The goal is not to chase trends but to identify opportunities that align with your financial objectives, risk tolerance, and investment horizon.

The first step in picking stocks is to clarify your investment goals. Are you seeking long-term growth, income through dividends, or a combination of these? Each goal influences the type of businesses you should consider. Long-term investors often prioritize growth stocks with the potential for significant appreciation over time, while income focused investors may lean toward companies with a history of consistent dividend payouts.

Understanding your risk tolerance is equally essential. Risk averse investors might gravitate toward established companies with stable earnings and market leadership, often referred to as blue chip stocks. These companies, such as Procter & Gamble or Walmart, have a history of weathering economic downturns while delivering steady returns. Conversely, risk tolerant investors may be drawn to industries, where the potential rewards are high with greater volatility.

When evaluating businesses to invest in, focus on sectors or industries that we understand. Investing in areas where we have personal or professional expertise gives us an edge, as we're better equipped to assess market trends and company fundamentals. For example, a software engineer might be more adept at evaluating technology companies, while someone with experience in agriculture could better understand opportunities in farming-related businesses. Warren Buffett, emphasizes staying within your "circle of competence." This principle encourages investors to focus on what they know, avoiding the pitfalls of venturing into unfamiliar territory.

Once you've identified a sector, narrow your search by looking for companies with sustainable competitive advantages. A competitive advantage allows a business to outperform its peers and maintain profitability over the long-term. These advantages may come in the form of strong brand recognition, proprietary technology, economies of scale, or a robust network effect. For example, Coca-Cola benefits from its global brand and distribution network, which make it difficult for competitors to replicate its success. Similarly, companies like Visa and

Business blueprint

Mastercard leverage network effects, where the value of their service increases as more people use it.

In any given industry, the competitive landscape often includes several players, yet only a small fraction emerges as dominant leaders. Out of five to eight competitors, it is typically one or two that rise to the top, achieving unparalleled success and shaping the market. These winners do not prevail by accident or luck; there are compelling reasons behind their dominance. As investors, the ability to uncover and understand these reasons is what distinguishes exceptional decision-making in the market.

The success of a business often lies in factors that may not be immediately visible on the surface. It could be their ability to innovate, creating products or services that redefine the industry. It might be operational efficiency that allows them to offer competitive pricing without sacrificing quality, or a powerful brand identity that builds customer loyalty and trust. Their market leadership could also stem from strategic decisions, such as choosing the right time to expand, entering underserved markets, or leveraging technology in ways their competitors cannot replicate.

Identifying these factors requires a mix of quantitative analysis and qualitative insight. It's not just about studying financial statements but understanding the vision of the management, the dynamics of the industry, and the adaptability of the business model. These insights reveal the critical edge that allows these companies to outpace their peers and secure their position at the top.

For investors, this process of discovery is both an art and a science. The more we train ourselves to recognize these qualities, the better positioned we are to invest in the businesses that have not only the potential to win but to sustain their victories in the long run. In doing so, we align ourselves with companies that don't just survive competition but thrive in it, creating lasting value for their shareholders.

Next, scrutinize a company's financial health by examining key financial metrics. Revenue growth is an essential indicator of whether the business is expanding, while profit margins reveal how efficiently it converts sales into earnings. For example, a company with consistent revenue growth and widening profit margins demonstrates operational strength and effective cost management. Additionally, analyze the company's balance sheet to assess its financial strength. A company with excessive debt relative to its equity may struggle during economic downturns, while those with manageable debt or net cash positions are better equipped to seize growth opportunities.

Cash flow is another critical metric. Free cash flow, the cash remaining after a company covers its operating expenses and capital expenditures, is a valuable measure of financial health. Companies with strong free cash flow can reinvest in growth initiatives, pay dividends, or reduce debt. Apple, for instance, generates substantial free cash flow, enabling it to fund innovation, reward shareholders, and maintain financial flexibility.

Understanding valuation is crucial in the stock-picking process. While growth and profitability are important, a stock's price relative to its intrinsic value determines whether it's a worthwhile investment. Common valuation metrics include the price-to-earnings (P/E) ratio, price-to-sales (P/S) ratio, and price-to-book (P/B) ratio. A low valuation relative to peers or historical averages may indicate an undervalued stock, though it's essential to consider the context. For example, a high P/E ratio might be justified for a rapidly growing tech company, while a low P/E ratio could signal challenges in a mature industry.

Real-world examples can illustrate these principles in action. Consider the case of Costco Wholesale Corporation (COST), a leader in the retail warehouse industry together with its subsidiaries, engages in the operation of membership warehouses in the United States, Puerto Rico, Canada, Mexico, Japan, the United Kingdom, Korea, Australia, Taiwan, China, Spain, France, Iceland, New Zealand, and Sweden. Costco has built a loyal customer base through its membership model, which drives recurring revenue. Its focus on low prices and high-quality private-label products has given it a competitive edge in the retail sector. Despite operating in a competitive market, Costco's strong financials, consistent growth, and disciplined management have made it a favorite among long-term investors.

Another example is Deere & Company (DE), a global leader in agricultural and construction equipment. Deere benefits from its strong brand reputation, innovative technology, and cyclical growth tied to global agricultural trends. The company's investments in precision agriculture technology have positioned it as a forward-looking player in the industry, appealing to investors seeking exposure to both traditional and cutting-edge opportunities.

For investors interested in emerging markets, Mercado Libre, Inc (MELI) offers a compelling case. As the leading e-commerce and fintech platform in Latin America, Mercado Libre has captured significant market share in a region with growing internet penetration and a rising middle class. The company's dual focus on online marketplaces and digital payment solutions provides multiple revenue streams, making it a standout player in an evolving market.

While identifying high-quality businesses is essential, timing your entry is equally important which we will dive deeper in the next chapter. The best companies are not always the best investments if purchased at the wrong price. Market corrections, industry specific challenges, or temporary setbacks can create opportunities to buy great companies at a discount. For instance, during the COVID-19 pandemic, many high-quality stocks experienced sharp declines, allowing patient investors to acquire them at attractive valuations.

A business we know very well should be concentrated rather than diversifying excessively into 10, 20, or more stocks. Diversification with 5 to 8 well researched stocks is often sufficient, as spreading your portfolio across too many stocks can lead to diluted returns and increased volatility. If a diversified portfolio is necessary, opting for ETFs with a reasonable expense ratio or an annual fee can be a more efficient choice earning average return than individual stocks, as it saves time on research while offering broad market exposure. Warren Buffett has emphasized that diversification is primarily a strategy for those who do not have the expertise to evaluate businesses effectively. He believes that if you can truly understand a few high-quality businesses, spreading investments across many companies may dilute potential returns. Buffett's approach to diversification is rooted in the idea that owning a concentrated portfolio of strong, well-understood companies is better than holding numerous stocks. This philosophy was highlighted when he mentioned that if someone in a local town owned just three businesses, like a cake shop or dry cleaner, they would be considered well diversified. Similarly, Buffett argues that holding a few, exceptional businesses can provide sufficient diversification if managed correctly

Investing is as much about psychology as it is about analysis. Emotional biases can cloud judgment, leading to poor decisions. Fear of missing out (FOMO) often drives investors to chase high flying stocks, while panic during market downturns can lead to premature selling. Developing a disciplined approach, guided by a clear investment thesis, helps mitigate these emotional pitfalls or Making mistakes in stock selection is an inevitable part of investing, making a mistake on stock selection doesn't means a 10% or more decline in the stock price. No matter how much research or analysis you conduct, there are always chances you may miss key details about a business. Over time, as you hold onto a stock, more information comes to light, and certain operational traits or business dynamics become clearer. As the years pass, you may begin to realize that some of the assumptions you made when you initially invested were wrong. This could lead you to conclude that you've made a mistake by choosing to invest in that stock. However, the situation becomes complicated when the stock price is trading significantly below the price you initially paid say, by 30% or more.

At this point, you're faced with a difficult decision: should we hold on to the stock in the hope that the price will eventually return to the breakeven point, or should we cut your losses and exit the position entirely? The temptation to hold may come from the hope that the market will eventually recognize the value of the business and push the stock price up. But this type of speculative thinking often carries substantial risk. If the business's future trajectory still seems uncertain, gambling on a rebound might only prolong your losses.

On the other hand, cutting out our losses and reallocating the capital to either support your existing portfolio or invest in a new opportunity can often be a better choice. The key here is to make a clear, informed assessment of the business's potential moving forward. If, after a thorough evaluation, you conclude that the stock's future growth prospects are unlikely to improve or that it has not recovered in a reasonable time frame, then accepting the loss may be the most prudent course of action. It's important to consider opportunity costs which refers to the returns you could have earned if you had invested your capital elsewhere. Holding onto a stock that has underperformed for an extended period not only ties up your capital but also prevents you from investing in better opportunities elsewhere.

Making this decision often comes down to your understanding of the business and its sector. If you are convinced that the business still has strong long-term prospects despite its current troubles, it may be worth holding onto the stock to break even. But if we're uncertain or believe that our capital could be better deployed elsewhere, cutting your losses and reinvesting might lead to better long-term outcomes. It's essential to approach these decisions without emotional attachment and with a focus on maximizing the overall returns of your portfolio.

Long-term thinking is a hallmark of successful investors. The stock market is inherently volatile in the short-term, but it rewards patience and persistence. Companies like Amazon and Tesla, which were once dismissed by skeptics, have delivered extraordinary returns to investors who believed in their long-term potential. Recognizing that value creation takes time can help investors avoid the trap of chasing short-term gains.

Investing is deeply personal, and aligning your investments with your values can make the journey not only financially rewarding but also emotionally fulfilling. Choosing to invest in ethical businesses allows you to support companies that reflect your beliefs and contribute positively to society. Whether it's businesses championing environmental sustainability, fair labor practices, or innovative solutions to global challenges, ethical investing gives your portfolio a sense of purpose beyond just monetary gains. By backing organizations that prioritize social responsibility and good governance, you actively participate in shaping a better future while potentially enjoying strong returns. It's a way to merge personal values with financial goals, turning your investments into a meaningful force for positive change.

Stock picking is not a one-time activity but an ongoing process. Monitoring your investments, staying informed about industry trends, and revisiting your investment thesis are essential to achieving long-term success. Even the best companies face challenges, and adapting to new information is key to maintaining a resilient portfolio.

In conclusion, picking the right stocks requires a blend of art and science. It involves identifying businesses with sustainable competitive advantages, robust financials, and attractive valuations while staying true to your investment goals and risk tolerance. By approaching the process with discipline, patience, and a willingness to learn, you can navigate the complexities of the stock market and build a portfolio that stands the test of time. Whether you're investing in established leaders or emerging disruptors, the principles of thoughtful stock selection remain the foundation of successful investing.

CHAPTER FOUR

MODEL OF EXCELLENCE

"I'm always looking at where I can make money, and I'm not afraid to taking risks."

-Carl Icahn

Investing in stocks requires a thorough understanding of business models, particularly those that align with our circle of competence. An attractive business model is one that, at first glance, reveals its potential through its products and services, revenue generation methods, risk factors, and aligned financials.

It is essential to understand how a business makes money. This involves examining the company's revenue streams, which could be diverse or concentrated. Investors need to assess whether the business has a solid economic foundation to withstand difficulties or a series of challenges. While a company's management can prepare for uncertainties in an uncertain market. This strategic preparedness is essential for maintaining investor confidence and ensuring the company's resilience and long-term success.

The stock market is a vast ecosystem with thousands of listed businesses, yet only a fraction of them achieves lasting success. Among these countless companies, some may seem easy to grasp based on their descriptions, while others remain elusive. However, for most investors, relying solely on the surface level understanding of a business is insufficient. Business models are complex, and markets are cyclical. Companies go through various phases, including growth, maturity, and sometimes decline. To mitigate the risk of investing in fully matured businesses with limited upside potential, it is crucial to seek opportunities in inefficient markets where the broader market has not yet recognized the true value of certain assets.

This concept can be illustrated through the analogy of real estate. Imagine a fully developed beachfront residential area, complete with amenities and is high demand. Properties in this area are likely priced at a premium or fully priced, with little room for significant appreciation. Investors eyeing this market might hope for rare discounts or distressed sales, but these opportunities are limited. Now consider a less glamorous but emerging neighborhood near a growing airport. Over the next 10 to 15 years, this area is poised for transformation, with new infrastructure, businesses, and residential developments making it highly desirable. At present, properties here may be undervalued, offering significant growth potential that could quadruple in value as the area develops. This is a clear example of market inefficiency, where current pricing does not yet reflect future potential.

Model of excellence

For retail investors, who often start with limited capital, the strategy should focus on uncovering such inefficiencies in the stock market. Efficient markets, where major analysts and institutional players dominate, often leave little room for retail investors to achieve outsized returns. These are the highly developed "beachfront" equivalents of the stock market companies that are fully priced, widely followed, and less likely to experience dramatic growth. On the other hand, inefficient markets those overlooked or undervalued offer opportunities for growth that require patience and foresight. Identifying these undervalued stocks and allowing time for them to grow into fully recognized and efficiently priced assets can result in substantial returns.

Investing in inefficiencies requires going beyond mere business descriptions and delving deeper into the fundamentals, industry dynamics, and growth potential. It demands an understanding of the market cycles, the ability to recognize undervalued assets, and the patience to hold investments until the broader market acknowledges their worth. This approach not only minimizes risk but also positions investors to capitalize on opportunities that others may overlook, setting the stage for long-term wealth creation.

Tesla, Inc. (TSLA) Initially, Tesla was viewed as a niche electric vehicle manufacturer, and its potential was underestimated by many traditional auto industry analysts. The company's stock traded inefficiently for years due to skepticism about its long-term profitability. As Tesla delivered consistent innovation and achieved scale, it attracted broader institutional interest. It is now one of the most closely tracked and efficiently priced stocks in the electric vehicle and renewable energy sectors.

Netflix, Inc. (NFLX) During its DVD rental phase and early streaming days, Netflix's value was overlooked by traditional media investors. The company was considered a speculative play in an unproven market. However, as the streaming model disrupted traditional television, Netflix's stock transitioned to efficiency, with its valuation reflecting its status as a dominant player in the entertainment industry.

Amazon.com, Inc. (AMZN) In the late 1990s and early 2000s, Amazon was considered a high-risk bet on e-commerce, with significant skepticism about its ability to scale and achieve profitability. As it expanded into cloud computing (AWS) and diversified its operations, the stock became a key component of institutional portfolios, moving into efficient pricing.

Nvidia Corporation. (NVDA) Initially viewed mainly as a graphics card company catering to gamers, Nvidia was undervalued by the broader market. Its potential in artificial intelligence, data centers, and autonomous vehicles was not fully appreciated until the past decade. As its strategic pivots succeeded, Nvidia became a leader in cutting-edge computing technology, with its stock now efficiently priced based on strong fundamentals.

Model of excellence

Domino's Pizza, Inc. (DPZ)For years, Domino's Pizza was regarded as a low-growth, traditional fast-food company. However, its strategic transformation, particularly its embrace of technology for online ordering and delivery logistics, turned it into a leader in the food-tech space. The stock moved from inefficiency to efficiency as the market recognized these innovations and their impact on earnings.

Shopify, Inc. (SHOP) During its early stages, Shopify was overlooked by many investors despite its innovative e-commerce platform and market potential. The stock traded at lower valuations as it was considered a niche business. Over time, as the company demonstrated consistent revenue growth, scalability, and the ability to compete with larger players, the market began to recognize its potential. The stock's valuation adjusted upward as it transitioned into a more efficient pricing zone recognized by institutional investors

Monster Beverage Corporation, (MNST)Previously known as Hansen's Natural, Monster Beverage was undervalued in its earlier years when it focused on niche natural sodas. Its transition to energy drinks and the success of the Monster Energy brand caused a dramatic shift. As revenue and market share soared, institutional investors took note, moving the stock from an inefficiently priced asset to one accurately reflecting its growing dominance in the energy drink market.

Block, Inc. (sq) Early in its public journey, Square faced skepticism regarding its ability to compete with established payment processors. Investors doubted its ability to expand beyond small businesses. Over time, Square diversified its offerings, including Cash App and cryptocurrency services, proving its scalability and innovation. This recognition corrected its undervaluation, pushing the stock into efficient market pricing territory.

Another critical aspect to consider is the risk factors associated with the business. What risk really means is not the percentage of money we have invested or a 50% of our capital is been wiped out. Risk taking is about understanding the circumstances of the business economics. For instance, consider a business with an excellent business model showing 15% year over year revenue growth and double-digit earnings. However, if accounts receivable is increasing year by year and the cash flow statement shows large outflows and constrained due to these rising accounts receivable, this represents a real risk for investors. Further study and research are needed to understand the management's strategy to tackle this deteriorating problem. Additionally, a business issuing debt year after year and running a deficit due to high interest payments poses significant risks. The key question is whether these risks are measurable. Understanding these risk factors allows investors to make informed decisions about the level of risk they are willing to accept. This comprehensive approach to evaluating business risks ensures that investments are based on thorough analysis rather than just surface level indicators. It is crucial to assess whether the business's revenue is increasing significantly to justify the continued issuance of debt. Investors need to determine if the debt issued is worth giving the business time to produce results. Furthermore, evaluating whether the business has enough working capital to run its operations smoothly is essential to avoid any permanent failure in its operations. This involves scrutinizing cash flow statements to ensure that the company can maintain its operations and meet its short-term obligations. By understanding these elements, investors can better gauge the potential risks and rewards associated with their investment and make more informed decisions about the business's long-term viability

The stock market is vast, with thousands of businesses to choose from. However, not all of them have sustainable business models. Many companies, despite initial success, eventually go bankrupt due to poor financial management, unsustainable business practices, or inability to adapt to market changes. This underscores the importance of thorough research, Proper Risk Management and careful selection of businesses with strong, resilient models.

Blockbuster filed for bankruptcy in 2010 due to the rise of digital streaming services and the decline of physical rental stores. The company struggled to adapt to changing consumer preferences and the emergence of competitors like Netflix.

Pier 1 Imports filed for bankruptcy in 2020, exacerbated by the COVID-19 pandemic. The company faced declining sales and mounting debt, which made it difficult to sustain its operations. Kodak filed for bankruptcy in 2012 as it struggled to transition from traditional film photography to digital photography. The company failed to innovate and keep up with technological advancements, leading to its decline.

Paper Source filed for bankruptcy in 2021 as a result of declining greeting card sales, exacerbated by the COVID-19 pandemic. The company faced significant debt and had to close several stores to manage its financial obligations.

Belk Department Store filed for bankruptcy in 2021 but managed to restructure its debt and emerge from bankruptcy within 24 hours. The company had to shed $450 million in debt and received $225 million in new capital to keep its 291 stores open.

Country Fresh, a supplier of ready-made meals and snacks, filed for bankruptcy in 2021 due to pandemic-related supply chain disruptions and business challenges. The company struggled with debt from packaging, logistics, shipping, and marketing contracts.

Party City filed for bankruptcy in 2022 due to declining sales and mounting debt. The company struggled to compete with online retailers and faced challenges in its physical store operations.

Model of excellence

Bed Bath & Beyond filed for bankruptcy in 2023 as it struggled with declining sales, high debt, and competition from online retailers. The company faced challenges in adapting to changing consumer preferences and the rise of e-commerce.

Rite Aid filed for bankruptcy in 2023 due to declining sales, high debt, and competition from larger pharmacy chains. The company struggled to maintain its market share and profitability.

Spirit Airlines filed for bankruptcy in November 2024 due to financial difficulties exacerbated by the COVID-19 pandemic and rising fuel costs.

Northvolt, a Swedish battery manufacturer, filed for bankruptcy in the United States in November 2024 due to supply chain disruptions and production delays.

BC Aventura, a contemporary furniture retailer, filed for bankruptcy in November 2024 due to declining sales and high debt levels.

Nordic Aviation Group filed for bankruptcy in November 2024 due to financial challenges and operational issues.

CareMax, a healthcare provider, filed for bankruptcy in November 2024 due to financial strain and operational difficulties.

Intrum, a Swedish financial services company, filed for bankruptcy in the United States in November 2024 due to mounting debt and declining revenue.

TGIF, a restaurant chain, filed for bankruptcy in November 2024 due to declining sales and high operational costs.

Accuride Corporation filed for bankruptcy in October 2024 due to financial difficulties and declining demand for its products.

Sally's Restaurant & Grill Sally's Restaurant & Grill filed for bankruptcy in October 2024 due to declining sales and high debt levels.

The College of Saint Rose filed for bankruptcy in October 2024 due to declining enrolment and financial challenges.

Tuesday Morning Corporation filed for bankruptcy in December 2022 due to declining sales and high debt levels. The company struggled to compete with online retailers and faced challenges in its physical store operations.

Core Scientific Inc filed for bankruptcy in December 2022 due to financial mismanagement and declining revenue. The company struggled to manage its debt and maintain profitability.

Model of excellence

Colicity Inc filed for bankruptcy in December 2022 due to financial mismanagement and declining revenue. The company faced challenges in its product development and market competition.

The key is to evaluate and invest in stocks with attractive business models within our circle of competence involves understanding the company's products and services, revenue generation methods, risk factors, aligned financial health and Management strategies that are on track to meet Business success and Investor Expectations. This approach not only helps in mitigating risks but also enhances the chances of achieving long-term investment success.

CHAPTER FIVE

ALIGNED AMBITIONS

Management is nothing more than motivating other people

-Lee Lacocca

The success of a business is deeply intertwined with the quality and effectiveness of its management team. This goes beyond just overseeing operations; it involves setting a strategic direction, fostering a positive company culture, and ultimately, driving financial performance. Understanding the nuances of leadership is particularly crucial when evaluating companies, where the influence of management can be more direct and impactful compared to larger corporations.

One effective way to gauge the effectiveness and integrity of a management team is by delving into financial statements. These documents are more than just numbers; they reflect the outcomes of management decisions, from revenue generation and cost management to investment strategies and financial planning. Through careful analysis, investors can discern patterns and insights into how well the management is steering the company. A consistent increase in revenue, well-managed expenses, and prudent capital allocation can signal a competent team. Conversely, erratic financial performance or excessive debt levels might suggest management struggles or poor strategic decisions.

Quantitative analysis serves as a powerful tool for uncovering insights into the management's ability to lead and grow a business. While management's vision and strategy are important, it is the numbers the financial results that truly validate whether their leadership is translating into real world success. No matter how impressive management claims to be, the numbers tell the ultimate story. By examining a company's financial performance over a period of five to ten years, investors can gain invaluable insights into how well management is aligned with the long-term goals of its investors. If a business has been consistently struggling with deficits year after year but is now turning around, increasing profitability, and strengthening its financial position, it should not go unnoticed. This is a sign that management has adapted and is executing a strategy that is beginning to pay off.

On the other hand, businesses that look attractive but fail to show signs of improvement in their financials should raise questions. Investors should not blindly invest in companies based solely on future projections or lofty ambitions without supporting data that can back up those expectations. The true test of management's quality comes through the lens of the financial statements. These documents provide the clearest picture of whether a business is on the path to success or whether the leadership is struggling to turn strategy into tangible outcomes. A business with consistent growth in revenue, profitability, and cash flow demonstrates that management's decisions are bearing fruit and aligning with the broader goals of long-term investors.

The financials reveal the underlying health of a business and provide a concrete foundation for any claims made about the company's future prospects. If the numbers support management's vision and show steady growth, investors can feel confident that their investment is in good hands. Ultimately, the quantitative analysis of financial data not only helps to confirm the strength of management but also provides reassurance to investors that the business is moving in the right direction and is a solid candidate for long-term commitment. The alignment of management's actions with the business's financial results is what truly solidifies the case for investing and sticking with the company over time.

Running a business and being an investor in one are fundamentally different endeavors, each requiring distinct mindsets and skills. As retail investors, our role doesn't demand the exhaustive operational responsibilities that come with managing a business like overseeing daily operations, leading large teams, or steering the organization through market challenges. Instead, we focus on understanding businesses from the outside, conducting thorough research, and making informed decisions about where to allocate our capital. While running a business is undeniably challenging, investing demands patience, strategic thinking, and the discipline to stick with decisions over the long-term.

The cornerstone of successful investing lies in selecting businesses led by exceptional management teams. Managers are the architects of a company's success, guiding employees and resources toward achieving organizational goals. They set the vision, make critical decisions, and execute strategies that can propel a company forward. As investors, when we align with businesses run by competent and visionary leaders, we increase the likelihood of seeing a strong return on our investments. Mediocre management, on the other hand, can lead to stagnation or decline, regardless of how promising the business model or industry may seem.

Investing, in essence, is placing our hard-earned money on the conviction that the business we choose will grow and succeed over time. The profits generated by a flourishing business create wealth not only for the company but also for its shareholders. This shared success highlights the interdependence between a business's operational achievements and an investor's financial gains. The right mindset as an investor is crucial: it helps us focus on long-term value creation rather than short-term market fluctuations. It also allows us to approach investments with clarity and purpose, aiming to make sound decisions that align with our financial goals.

Investing in stocks is not merely about analyzing market trends or financial metrics; it's also about understanding the people at the helm of the company. The alignment between management's ambition and investors' goals is crucial. When both parties share a common vision, it creates a powerful synergy that can propel the company to new heights. Investors must be confident that the management team is not only capable but also trustworthy and committed to long-term value creation, rather than short-term gains. which may lack the extensive track records of their larger counterparts. Their growth potential often hinges on the vision, skill, and integrity of their leaders.

Take Crocs Inc., for instance. Once a niche brand, it underwent a remarkable transformation under its leadership. The strategic decisions to embrace innovative marketing strategies and capitalize on consumer trends like comfort focused footwear drove impressive growth. The management team identified and seized opportunities that larger competitor overlooked, highlighting the crucial role of strategic leadership in unlocking value.

In the small cap stock universe, consider Axon Enterprise Inc. (AXON) a company specializing in public safety technology. The leadership's commitment to innovation has enabled Axon to establish itself as a pioneer in its field, despite competition from larger players. By maintaining a strong focus on research and development and nurturing relationships with law enforcement agencies, Axon has consistently demonstrated the importance of management in driving a small company toward long-term success.

Following earnings calls is another valuable approach for investors. These calls provide a platform for management to communicate directly with investors and analysts, offering insights into their strategic thinking, future plans, and how they respond to challenges. The tone, confidence, and clarity with which management presents and addresses questions can be very revealing. Investors should pay attention to how management explains unexpected challenges or justifies underperformance. Are they transparent, or do they confuse the issues? This can reveal whether the leadership is candid and trustworthy qualities that are particularly crucial for companies still establishing their reputation.

Earnings calls for companies like Etsy Inc. (ETSY) a mid-cap e-commerce platform, highlight the impact of transparent communication. Etsy's management has consistently outlined clear strategies for scaling the platform while maintaining its unique appeal as a marketplace for handmade and vintage items. This balance between growth and preserving the company's core identity reflects the importance of thoughtful and transparent leadership. Etsy's success in carving out a distinct niche in a competitive industry can largely be attributed to its leadership's ability to align operational strategies with its vision.

Investors can also gain valuable insights by reviewing employee feedback on platforms like Glassdoor. These platforms can offer a glimpse into the company's internal culture and the effectiveness of its leadership from the perspective of those who work there. Consistently negative reviews might indicate issues with management that could eventually impact the company's performance. Conversely, positive reviews often reflect a healthy corporate culture, which is conducive to long-term success.

Consider the small cap company Planet Fitness, Inc. (PLNT) Employee reviews reveal a generally positive workplace culture, emphasizing inclusivity and empowerment, values championed by its leadership. This culture has translated into strong customer loyalty and robust business growth, with the management team steering the company toward sustainable expansion through franchise-based operations. Understanding such qualitative factors can provide investors with a fuller picture of a company's potential.

Looking into the backgrounds of CEOs and other top executives can also provide valuable insights. Understanding their track record at previous employers, their reputation in the industry, and their professional achievements can help predict how they might perform in their current role. As the saying goes, "history often repeats itself." If a business has been involved in fraudulent activities and faced penalties, there's a risk that similar issues might arise again, especially if the same management team is in place. While past behaviors don't guarantee future actions, it offers critical context for evaluating potential risks.

A compelling example is the turnaround story of Chipotle Mexican Grill, Inc. (CMG) led by its CEO, Brian Niccol. Before joining Chipotle, Niccol spearheaded Taco Bell's transformation, emphasizing innovation and marketing. His track record gave investors' confidence in his ability to lead Chipotle through its recovery phase. Under Niccol's leadership, the company embraced technology, revamped its menu, and rebuilt its reputation, highlighting how the right management can make a profound difference.

The small cap company Enphase Energy, Inc. (ENPH) is another case worth noting. The company's CEO, Badri Kothandaraman, has a background in engineering and operational excellence. His leadership has helped Enphase pivot toward renewable energy solutions, focusing on solar microinverters. Kothandaraman's strategic decisions have propelled the company into the mid cap space, demonstrating the importance of visionary management in scaling a small business.

Moreover, the impact of management extends beyond individual companies. Entire industries have been reshaped by visionary leaders who dared to challenge conventions. Consider the impact of Elon Musk on the electric vehicle industry. While Tesla is a large cap company today, it began as a relatively small player. Musk's bold vision and relentless drive have transformed not only Tesla but also the global perception of electric vehicles. Such transformative leadership highlights the potential of companies led by forward thinking individuals.

However, it's important to note that not all bold leadership leads to success. Overconfidence or misjudgments can lead to significant setbacks. For example, WeWork's failed IPO serves as a cautionary tale of how a charismatic leader's ambitious vision, when ungrounded in reality, can result in financial disaster. This underscores the importance of balancing ambition with prudence when evaluating management teams.

In conclusion, the role of management in the success of a business cannot be overstated. Effective, aligned, and transparent leadership is fundamental to driving a company toward its goals. For investors, understanding the nuances of management's decisions and behaviors, through financial statements, earnings calls, employee feedback, and the backgrounds of key executives, is essential for making informed investment decisions. This due diligence helps in identifying not just profitable opportunities but also in mitigating risks associated with poor or unethical management practices. By focusing on the traits and track records of management teams, investors can better align their portfolios with companies that are not only financially sound but also well led and poised for sustainable success.

The examples of small cap and mid cap companies such as Axon Enterprise, Enphase Energy, Etsy, and Planet Fitness demonstrate that strong management can significantly impact a company's trajectory. Investors who take the time to understand and evaluate the leadership teams behind these businesses are better positioned to identify opportunities that align with their investment goals and risk tolerance. This emphasizes the critical role of leadership in investment success and provides a framework for evaluating management quality in companies of all sizes.

Through these insights, investors can approach their stock selection with greater confidence, ensuring that their portfolios are not only financially robust but also aligned with principles of strong governance and ethical leadership.

Whether investing in established mid cap firms or emerging small-cap businesses, the quality of management remains a decisive factor in achieving sustainable long-term returns.

By carefully considering these factors, investors can make more informed decisions about the management teams they choose to support. Ultimately, a strong management team is a valuable asset that can drive long-term growth and shareholder value.

Furthermore, it's important to note that the role of management extends beyond the traditional boundaries of the company. Effective leaders can inspire innovation, foster collaboration, and create a positive impact on society as a whole. By aligning their business goals with broader societal needs, management teams can drive sustainable growth and contribute to a more equitable and sustainable future.

CHAPTER SIX

TIMING PLAYBOOK

"The market can stay irrational longer than you can stay solvent"

-John Maynard Keynes

Market cycles, driven by supply and demand dynamics, are fundamental to understanding when to buy stocks. During optimistic periods, prices are pushed up as more investors buy, while in pessimistic periods, prices decline due to selling. Market cycles consist of four stages: accumulation, mark-up, distribution, and mark-down.

In the financial markets, there will come a point where even the most optimistic investors will lose their steam, unable to push prices up any further. As a result, the available cash reserves of these investors will become depleted. Conversely, during times of pessimism, savvy investors will seize the opportunity to purchase stocks at substantial discounts. These opportunistic investors, armed with cash reserves, will capitalize on the presented opportunities, driving prices up. Gradually, the market will recognize the underlying value of these businesses, leading to an upward adjustment in prices. Overall, market dynamics exhibit a cyclical nature where the interplay between optimism and pessimism, combined with the availability of cash reserves, influences stock prices and the perceived value of underlying businesses.

The accumulation stage occurs after a market has bottomed out, with informed investors beginning to buy. Despite negative sentiment, this phase is characterized by low prices and low trading volumes. The mark-up phase follows, where prices start to rise as more investors become aware of the improving fundamentals and begin to buy, driving prices higher. This stage often sees increased trading volumes and a rise in market optimism.

Next is the distribution phase, where those who bought during accumulation start to sell. Prices may still rise or stabilize, but the rate of increase slows, and trading volumes remain high. Finally, the mark-down phase begins as more investors realize that the market has peaked, leading to widespread selling and declining prices.

Patience and disciplined investment strategies are crucial in navigating these cycles. During optimistic periods, it's essential to resist the urge to chase high prices and instead focus on the underlying value of the business. Investing at all-time highs can be risky, but it can also present opportunities for future gains if the business's fundamentals remain strong.

For example, consider a mid-cap stock in the technology sector with a market cap of $10 billion. If it experiences a 5% price increase, it requires significant trading volume, but the key is understanding whether this rise is driven by genuine improvements in the business or merely market speculation. Investing in such a stock after thorough research ensures that you are betting on the company's long-term potential rather than short-term price movements.

Similarly, during pessimistic periods, it's important to stay calm and focus on the business's fundamentals. A sell-off might result from short-term bad news or broader economic issues, but this doesn't necessarily mean the business is in trouble or closing it's doors. As this happens, the savvy investors start to see the real value of these companies. In the end, the back-and-forth between optimism and pessimism, along with having cash reserves, influences stock prices and shows the true worth of businesses. If you have done your research and believe in the company's long-term prospects, these periods can present buying opportunities.

For instance, if the same mid-cap technology stock falls 30% due to quarterly earnings miss or lose a significant client, but its long-term growth prospects remain intact, this could be an opportunity to add to your position at a lower price. Maintaining a cash reserve is essential to capitalize on such opportunities without having to sell other investments at a loss.

Understanding market cycles and being patient can help you make informed investment decisions. By focusing on the underlying value of businesses and avoiding emotional reactions to market fluctuations, you can navigate the stock market more effectively and achieve long-term investment success.

Why hold the stock when the price is at an all-time high? This question often plagues investors, especially when market conditions are buzzing with excitement and anxiety. The role of investment decisions in buying, selling, holding, adding into a stock cannot be overstated. Picture this: the market reaches new heights, news outlets are ablaze with predictions, and perhaps even your family members are urging you to cash in your profits. It is in these moments that the need for introspection becomes paramount. Reflect on why you invested in that stock in the first place. Did you spend countless hours researching and pondering before making the purchase? The initial decision to invest likely stemmed from the long-term prospects of the business, its solid foundation, and the positive impact its products or services bring to the world. The goal was not a fleeting 10x return, but a commitment to a business whose mission aligns with ethical practices, value to customers, and returns to shareholders.

The annual review of business economics and management integrity is essential in making informed decisions about holding, adding to, or selling a stock. Imagine the business you invested in is now at an all-time high, presenting you with a significant gain. How should you approach this scenario? You should consider holding or even adding to your position if the business continues to exhibit robust economic fundamentals and management integrity. Even after experiencing a 10x gain or a significant loss in share price. If the business maintains it's core strength and business economics have significantly improved, making the company more attractive to investors and showing strong future potential then you should consider holding onto the winning investment. However, if the business's economic situation starts to deteriorate permanently rather temporary, it may be time to consider selling your position and moving on to more promising investments. An annual review of the business economics and management integrity can help you make informed decisions about whether to continue holding or to sell your stock. This brings us to the importance of understanding the intrinsic value of the underlying business and avoiding impulsive decisions based on temporary gains or losses.

Take, for instance, Warren Buffett's purchase of See's Candies. Which he has held the business dearly as long as it maintained the required standards of economics and integrity. The decision to buy, sell, hold, or add more to your investment portfolio hinges on a strict annual review of the business. As a publicly traded entity, this transparency allows investors to align their ambitions with the company's long-term success, rather than treating stock trading as a hobby.

The core of investing lies in the ability to stay committed to a well-researched decision despite the noise of market fluctuations. When the stock price reaches an all-time high, it might seem tempting to liquidate and lock in profits, but this is where discipline and a clear understanding of your investment thesis come into play. Your investment journey did not start with a mere hope for quick gains; it began with a thorough evaluation of the company's potential and its place in your portfolio. This foundation should guide your decisions, especially when the market is at its peak.

Holding onto a stock at its all-time high requires a steadfast belief in the business's continued success. It's essential to remember that market prices are often driven by short-term sentiments and external factors that may not necessarily reflect the company's actual performance. By focusing on the intrinsic value of the business and its long-term prospects, investors can make more rational decisions that align with their overall investment strategy.

Moreover, the pressure to sell can come from various sources, including media hype, social influence, and personal biases. It's crucial to distinguish between noise and valuable information. News outlets thrive on sensationalism, and the constant barrage of market predictions can lead to anxiety and impulsive decisions. Similarly, family and friends may have their own opinions and fears about the stock market, but their advice may not always align with your investment goals. It's important to stay grounded in your own research and convictions.

Another factor to consider is the potential for future growth. Just because a stock has reached an all-time high doesn't mean it has peaked in terms of its growth potential. The company may have new products, innovations, or market expansions that could drive further growth. Evaluating these factors requires a deep understanding of the business and staying updated with its developments. This ongoing analysis helps in making informed decisions about whether to hold, add to, or sell your position.

Furthermore, reinvesting dividends and capital gains can amplify long-term returns. By holding onto a stock that pays regular dividends and reinvesting those payments, investors can benefit from compounding returns over time. This strategy not only enhances the growth of your investment but also provides a steady income stream that can be reinvested or used for other purposes.

Holding a concentrated portfolio, rather than a diversified one, involves investing a significant portion of your funds in a limited number of stocks. This approach can amplify gains but also increases exposure to market volatility. Therefore, it's crucial that the money you invest in a concentrated portfolio comes from surplus savings or disposable income. It should never be funds allocated for essential expenses like your children's school fees, living standards, or other necessary costs. By ensuring that only surplus funds are invested, you protect your financial stability and safeguard your family's well-being against potential market volatility.

In conclusion, holding a stock when the price is at an all-time high requires a combination of discipline, informed decision-making, and a long-term perspective. Reflecting on the original purpose of your investment, conducting regular evaluations of the business's fundamentals, and avoiding impulsive decisions are key to successful investing. The market's highs and lows should not deter you from your investment thesis but rather reinforce the importance of staying committed to your well-researched decisions. By focusing on the intrinsic value of the business and its long-term prospects, investors can navigate the complexities of the stock market with confidence and achieve their financial goals.

CHAPTER SEVEN

SAFETY NET STRATEGIES

"When you change the way you look at things, the things you look at change"

-Wayne Dyer

Knowing the price of a stock but not being able to identify its value is indeed a crisis for any investor. It's like navigating through a dense forest without a clear path. You might have a sense of direction, but without a detailed understanding of the terrain, you could easily find yourself lost. The concept of the margin of safety is a cornerstone of value investing and is crucial in navigating the complexities of the stock market. It acts as a buffer between the intrinsic value of a stock and its market price, offering a cushion against errors in estimation and unforeseen market downturns.

In the previous chapter, we emphasized the importance of thoroughly understanding the business before making any investment. This fundamental principle cannot be overstated. Without a comprehensive grasp of the business and its financials, investors are at a significant disadvantage, unable to accurately value a company. This understanding encompasses knowing the industry in which the business operates, the competitive landscape, and the company's unique strengths and weaknesses.

The industry context is essential in helping investors apply valuation metrics more effectively. Various metrics, such as Price to Sales (P/S), Price to Earnings (P/E), Price to Free Cash Flow (P/FCF), and Price to Book (P/B), play crucial roles in evaluating a business. However, their relevance can vary significantly depending on the industry dynamics and the specific circumstances of the company in question

Valuing a business is not about adhering to a secret formula but rather about integrating both qualitative and quantitative aspects. A company might present a great valuation but operate in an industry with uncertain growth prospects. In such cases, even if the price paid reflects the intrinsic value, the return might not justify the investment if the growth potential is limited.

Growth and value are inherently intertwined. Investing in a mediocre business at a low valuation might not yield the desired returns. Instead, one should aim for high-quality businesses available at fair or low valuations, which offer both value and growth potential. The challenge lies in avoiding the bias towards value alone and considering the growth prospects of the business.

Investors often fall into the trap of being biased by low valuations, overlooking the lack of growth potential. It is crucial to recognize that a business trading at a low valuation might be doing so for a reason, such as poor growth prospects or

Safety net strategies

underlying industry issues. On the other hand, exceptional businesses often trade at high valuations. While it is rare and challenging, it is still possible to find those that are undervalued with great growth prospects. This underscores the importance of thorough due diligence to understand the true value and growth potential of any investment.

Identifying businesses with low valuations and strong business fundamentals, or those that are fairly valued with excellent growth potential, requires diligence and a deep understanding of the business and its industry. The key is to use valuation to your advantage, seeking exceptional results rather than settling for mediocrity.

To illustrate the concept of the margin of safety, let us consider a practical example. Suppose you identify a company with strong financial health, a robust business model, and a competitive edge in its industry. After thorough analysis, you estimate its intrinsic value based on its total market capitalization to be $1 billion. This intrinsic value might be derived from various factors, including the company's future prospects, revenue, profitability, and tangible assets.

For instance, the company might generate an annual revenue of $500 million and possess tangible assets worth $600 million. Using these figures, along with an appropriate valuation multiple, you estimate that the fair market capitalization should be $1 billion. However, the current market capitalization of the company is only $700 million. The difference of $300 million represents your margin of safety, providing a buffer against potential errors in your analysis or unforeseen market conditions.

This margin of safety allows you to invest with greater confidence, knowing that even if your estimations are slightly off, the risk of significant loss is minimized. It also provides an opportunity to achieve substantial gains if the market eventually recognizes the company's true value. By focusing on the overall market capitalization and comparing it with the company's revenue and tangible assets, you can make a more informed investment decision.

This margin of safety allows you to invest with greater confidence, knowing that even if your estimations are slightly off, the risk of significant loss is minimized. It also provides an opportunity to achieve substantial gains if the market eventually recognizes the company's true value.

One of the key challenges in applying the margin of safety is accurately determining the intrinsic value of a stock. This requires a combination of financial analysis, industry knowledge, and a bit of intuition. The process involves evaluating a company's financial statements, understanding its business model, and industry trends.

Additionally, investors must be wary of overconfidence and ensure that their valuation assumptions are realistic and based on solid data. A generous margin of safety can compensate for some errors, but it should not be an excuse for sloppy analysis.

Several tools and techniques can assist investors in valuing a business and determining the margin of safety. These include:

Discounted Cash Flow (DCF) Analysis is one of the most fundamental and widely used valuation techniques. It involves estimating the present value of a company's future cash flows. This method is rooted in the principle that the value of a business is essentially the sum of its future cash flows, discounted back to their present value using an appropriate discount rate. The process begins with forecasting the company's free cash flows for a certain period, typically five to ten years. These future cash flows are then discounted using the company's weighted average cost of capital (WACC) to account for the time value of money and the inherent risks associated with the business. The result is the present value of these future cash flows, which provides an estimate of the company's intrinsic value. It requires careful estimation of future cash flows and an appropriate discount rate, making it a technique that demands both analytical rigor and a sound understanding of the company's business model and growth prospects.

Comparable Company Analysis, on the other hand, takes a more relative approach. Instead of focusing solely on the target company's intrinsic value, this method involves comparing the valuation multiples of similar companies within the same industry. Commonly used multiples include Price to Earnings (P/E), Enterprise Value to EBITDA (EV/EBITDA), and Price to Sales (P/S). By analyzing these multiples, investors can gauge whether a stock is overvalued or undervalued relative to its peers. This market-based perspective helps in understanding how the market values companies with similar operational and financial characteristics. The key to this analysis lies in selecting truly comparable companies, which share similar growth rates, profit margins, and risk profiles.

Precedent Transactions Analysis adds another layer of insight, particularly useful in understanding the premiums paid for control and the strategic value attributed to companies by acquirers. This method involves analyzing the valuations of similar companies involved in recent mergers and acquisitions. By examining these transactions, investors can gain insights into the market conditions at the time of the deals, the strategic rationale behind them, and the valuation multiples applied. This helps in estimating the value of a company based on real-world transactions, reflecting what buyers are willing to pay under specific market conditions.

Asset-Based Valuation, as the name suggests, focuses on the value of a company's assets. This approach is often used for asset-heavy industries where the value of physical and tangible assets plays a significant role. The process involves assessing the value of a company's tangible and intangible assets, net of liabilities, to determine its net asset value (NAV). Tangible assets include physical properties like real estate, machinery, and inventory, while intangible assets encompass things like patents, trademarks, and goodwill. This method is particularly useful for companies undergoing liquidation or facing financial distress, where the asset value can provide a floor for the company's valuation.

Each of these valuation methods offers unique insights and has its own set of advantages and limitations. By integrating multiple approaches, investors can develop a more comprehensive understanding of a company's value, thereby enhancing their investment decisions. Using a combination of DCF,

Safety net strategies

Comparable Company Analysis, Precedent Transactions, and Asset-Based Valuation can provide a well-rounded view, balancing the intrinsic, relative, and asset-based perspectives. This multifaceted approach helps in minimizing errors and capturing the true value of a business from different angles.

Incorporating the margin of safety into your investment strategy requires discipline and patience. It is important to resist the temptation to chase high-flying stocks and instead focus on identifying undervalued opportunities with a sufficient margin of safety.

Understanding and applying the margin of safety is a fundamental aspect of value investing. It provides a cushion against errors in valuation and market volatility, allowing investors to make more informed and confident decisions. By thoroughly understanding the business, considering both qualitative and quantitative factors, and applying disciplined valuation techniques, investors can increase their chances of achieving exceptional results while minimizing risks. Remember, the goal is not just to find undervalued stocks but to invest in high-quality businesses with strong growth potential at reasonable prices. This balance between value and growth is the key to successful investing.

CHAPTER EIGHT

MONEY MATTERS

"Don't tell me where your priorities are, show me where you spend your money and I'll tell you what they are."

-James W. Frick

Warren Buffett is credited with the phrase "accounting is the language of business." Understanding financial statements is crucial as they provide a comprehensive view of a company's financial health.

We will discuss three parts of the financial statement: Income Statement, Balance Sheet, and Cash Flow Statement.

When considering investing in a business, certain fundamental traits are non-negotiable, and one of the most critical indicators is revenue generation. Revenue represents the initial proof of success, as it reflects the acceptance and demand for the company's products or services. A business consistently bringing in revenue demonstrates its ability to engage the market, meet customer needs, and maintain operational stability. This revenue stream becomes a primary gauge for investors to assess the market share and growth potential of the company. A robust revenue trajectory not only establishes the company's success but also strengthens investor conviction in its long-term prospects.

However, revenue alone should not be the sole determinant of a company's potential. It acts as a starting point for a deeper analysis. For investors venturing into businesses within industries they thoroughly understand, the revenue provides valuable context. But when a business generates limited or declining revenue, it calls for further scrutiny. Investors must evaluate whether this shortfall stems from temporary challenges, such as economic downturns or operational inefficiencies, or from more significant structural problems within the company. Temporary setbacks, if addressed strategically, can be resolved, leading to recovery and growth. However, systemic or permanent issues, such as a flawed business model or irreversible industry decline, could signal a poor investment decision.

The decision-making process becomes even more critical when the investor has a strong conviction about the industry's future potential. If a company's revenue underperforms, the investor must objectively question their assumptions about the industry itself. Have market conditions shifted, or is there a fundamental misunderstanding of the business's competitive positioning? Alternatively, if the industry remains viable, the company's problems might be specific and solvable, providing an opportunity for a turnaround. Understanding these nuances helps investors avoid mistaking short-term setbacks for long-term failure and ensures informed investment decisions.

Ultimately, revenue serves as a crucial metric and without a stable and growing revenue base, the survival of a business is inevitably at risk., but it must be evaluated within the broader context of industry trends, market positioning, and operational performance. This comprehensive approach allows investors to identify businesses capable of overcoming challenges and delivering sustained success.

A year-over-year revenue growth of 5% can be significant depending on the business model and industry. It serves as proof that the company's offerings resonate with its target audience and validates its business strategy. Stable revenue generation becomes a cornerstone for further study and consideration for investment. However, revenue alone doesn't paint the full picture. The income statement reveals how effectively the management transforms this revenue into profit, highlighting operational efficiency and the company's ability to optimize costs.

Examining gross margin, operating margin, and profit margin trends over a 5–10-year period helps investors assess the management's resilience and capacity to navigate challenges. Large enterprises face the complex task of balancing expenses while maximizing profit, and a consistent ability to maintain or improve margins is a testament to exceptional leadership. When a company transitions from negative to positive profit margins, it showcases remarkable adaptability and strategic prowess.

One-time spikes in revenue or profit are insufficient to guarantee sustained success. A thorough analysis of income statement components like cost of goods sold, operating expenses, and overall profitability is necessary to gauge the robustness of a business model. Revenue generation validates the market demand for the business, but turning that revenue into sustainable profits requires managerial expertise. Investors should rely on long-term data to ensure the business they're evaluating demonstrates not only resilience but also the capacity to consistently create value for its stakeholders.

To truly understand a business's potential, one must dive deeper into its revenue structure, exploring the various channels through which it generates income. Analyzing how a company earns its revenue provides critical insights into its operational model and strategic focus. Investigating the geographic reach of the business reveals the scope of its market presence and highlights whether there is untapped potential for expansion into new regions or territories. Identifying the segments of the business that contribute most significantly to revenue, as well as those that are underperforming, allows for an informed evaluation of where the company's strengths and weaknesses lie.

Research and development efforts are equally pivotal. A business that invests in innovation demonstrates a forward-thinking approach, introducing new products or services to maintain relevance and capture market demand. This is an essential factor in sustaining long-term growth and fending off competition. On the other hand, the allocation of revenue toward sales and marketing requires careful scrutiny. While a strategic investment in these areas can amplify growth, excessive expenditure may signal inefficiency or desperation to maintain a foothold in the market.

Understanding these dimensions equips investors with the foresight to assess the future trajectory of the business. It becomes possible to predict whether the company is positioned for growth, stagnation, or decline. A balanced approach, where revenue streams are diverse, geographical presence is optimized, and expenditures are justified, often signals a well-managed business with promising prospects. By thoroughly examining these aspects, investors can make decisions rooted in deep analysis rather than speculation, fostering a greater likelihood of aligning their investments with enduring success.

A prime example is Visa, Inc. (V), operates as a payment technology company in the United States and internationally. Which has increased its revenue year by year, currently trailing at an impressive $36 Billion. This growth highlights the company's efficiency in generating more revenue and capturing market share. Analyzing their revenue can provide insights into the business's growth trajectory, such as whether their products or services are recurring or one-time sales, which countries the business serves, and what plans there are for expansion into underserved markets. Additionally, examining the competitive landscape can reveal what sets their products and services apart from competitors, whether it be through sales and marketing or research and development.

Metrics such as gross profit margins, operating margins, and profit margins provide insight into how efficiently management is running the business and converting it into profitability. Effective cost management is a crucial factor in business success. Currently, Visa, Inc. (V) has a gross profit margin of 98%, an operating margin of 67%, and a profit margin of 54%. These figures illustrate the company's ability to manage its costs effectively, contributing to its overall success. The gross profit margin reflects the efficiency of production and pricing strategies, the operating margin indicates the company's operational efficiency, and the profit margin shows the overall profitability after all expenses. These metrics are essential for assessing the financial health and operational performance of the company.

By understanding the income statement, it shows how strong the business is positioned in the market in terms of their market share and growth opportunities, and the margins help us understand the competitive advantage the business has in turning the revenue into profits for the business's sustainability and future success.

~

Understanding a company's balance sheet is akin to comprehending one's personal finances. Peter Lynch's quote, "Never invest in a company without understanding its finances. The biggest losses in stocks come from companies with poor balance sheets," serves as a timeless reminder for investors. The balance sheet, much like a personal net worth statement, reveals whether a company owns more than it owes. A positive net worth demonstrates financial stability and room for growth, while a negative one highlights potential vulnerabilities that could undermine a company's future.

In personal finance, assessing our net worth helps us navigate critical decisions such as debt repayment, savings strategies, and long-term planning. Similarly, a company's balance sheet is essential for evaluating its financial health, operational resilience, and strategic potential. It sheds light on critical metrics like liquidity, debt levels, and asset efficiency, enabling investors to assess whether the company can weather economic downturns, fund innovation, and seize market opportunities. A robust balance sheet is more than a snapshot; it is an indicator of long-term viability, showcasing the company's ability to adapt to market changes and sustain its operations even during turbulent times.

For businesses, a strong balance sheet means access to capital, reduced financial stress, and the ability to outpace competitors. It reflects prudent management decisions and proactive strategies to balance assets and liabilities effectively. Conversely, poor balance sheet management can jeopardize a company's future, signaling higher risk for investors. Companies with high debt-to-equity ratios or insufficient liquidity may struggle to meet obligations, invest in growth, or withstand industry challenges.

Investors who neglect the balance sheet risk exposing themselves to unstable businesses, often leading to significant losses. A well-maintained balance sheet is not just an accounting statement but a testament to the company's commitment to sustainable and strategic financial management. It provides the clarity and assurance that investors need to make informed, confident decisions, aligning their investments with companies poised for long-term success. By delving deeply into a company's balance sheet, investors can uncover its potential, evaluate management's competency, and ensure alignment with their own financial goals

Consider the case of Bed Bath & Beyond, Inc. (BBBYQ) together with its subsidiaries, operates a chain of retail stores. which closed its doors in April 2023. In 2017, the company had assets worth $7 billion and liabilities of $4 billion, with total debt at $1.49 billion. Over the following years, from 2018 to 2020, the balance sheet showed a deterioration in assets, an increase in liabilities, and a growing debt. By 2021 and into 2022, it became evident that the company's chance of survival was in question. This example highlights the importance of closely monitoring a company's financial statements. As investors, we should hold these financial documents dearly, as they provide us with the edge to manage our risk in the businesses we invest.

In conclusion, the balance sheet is an essential tool for understanding a company's financial health and its potential for long-term survival. By analyzing the components of the balance sheet, investors can make informed decisions and better manage their investment risks.

~

"When it comes to investing, you need to have an edge in cash flows, not accounting profits. Cash flows are hard facts, whereas accounting profits can be manipulated." - Howard marks

Money matters

Business success is investors' success. Cash flow is fundamental to understanding the inflows and outflows of cash within a business, and more importantly, how that cash is being utilized to generate value for shareholders and the business itself. The cash flow statement offers a detailed picture of whether a business is making the necessary adjustments for growth, such as acquisitions, investments in other securities to source additional income, capital expenditure, retaining shareholder value through dividends or share repurchases, and maintaining cash reserves.

As investors, especially retail investors who hold a small percentage of the business, we may have limited influence over the board of directors' decisions. However, we do have the freedom to invest in businesses where our interests align with the management and the board. The cash flow statement helps us gauge whether management is making decisions that enhance the business's value and sustainability. This includes monitoring free cash flow (operating cash flow minus capital expenditure) and observing activities like acquisitions, dividend payout ratios, share repurchases, debt repayment, investments in other securities, increases in capital expenditure, and net cash flow of cash and cash equivalents.

For instance, Danaos Corporation (DAC), which provides container and dry bulk vessel services in Australia, Asia, and Europe, ended the year 2022 with significant cash flow metrics. The company reported cash from operations of $935 million, capital expenditure of $199 million, and free cash flow of $736 million. Will our interest align with the management's decisions? A dividend payout ratio of 10%, while the company still retains enough cash to avoid constraints, A share repurchase yield of 0.40% indicates the business is buying back its shares - favoring investors by preventing dilution of shareholder equity. Additionally, the net debt repaid for the year was $864 million, showcasing the management's commitment to improving the balance sheet's future sustainability. With $247 million invested in securities and a positive net cash flow of cash and cash equivalents adding $137 million to the balance sheet, it is clear that the management is focused on increasing shareholder value and the overall business value.

In conclusion, the cash flow statement is a critical tool for understanding how a business manages its cash resources. By analyzing cash inflows and outflows, and how the cash is used for growth and sustainability, investors can make informed decisions that align with their interests and the long-term success of the business.

Healthcare Service Group, Inc. (HCSG) provides management, administrative, and operating services to the housekeeping, laundry, linen, facility maintenance, and dietary service departments of nursing homes, retirement complexes, rehabilitation centers, and hospitals in the United States. The company's Dividend payout ratio had become unsustainable, meaning it was paying out more in dividends than it was earning in profits. In November 2022, Healthcare Service Group, Inc. (HCSG) suspended its dividend payments due to concerns about its financial sustainability. This decision was made to preserve cash

Money matters

and invest in the business to improve its long-term financial health.

There is no point in investors receiving dividends when the business's financials are in ruin. Certain decisions should be made by management to improve the business's financials and sustainability, resulting in business success and benefits for shareholders. This is where retail investors have the opportunity to make decisions to invest in businesses where their interests align with the management.

CHAPTER NINE

MONOPOLY

"An investment in knowledge pays the best interest."

-Benjamin Franklin

I used to play Monopoly quite often, and one fine day, I found myself in an online multiplayer match that would fundamentally change my approach to Investing. My opponent had an unusual strategy that intrigued me: she passed on purchasing properties and simply collected her $200 salary each time she passed "Go." On the other hand, I was following my usual aggressive approach, buying every property I could land on and burning through my cash reserves rapidly. As a result, my opponent accumulated a substantial pile of cash while I was left with many properties but no cash reserve.

From the beginning of the game, my strategy was clear. I believed in the power of property ownership, the consistent income from rent, and the dominance that owning multiple sets could bring. Each time I landed on a property; I purchased it without a second thought. This left me with little cash in hand but a significant portion of the board under my control. It was a tactic that had worked well for me in the past, but this game was different.

As I bought properties, I noticed that my opponent was doing something quite unexpected. She moved around the board, collecting her salary but never investing in properties. At first, I thought this was a novice mistake or perhaps she was unfamiliar with the game's strategic depth. However, as the turns progressed, I realized that her cash reserves were growing significantly while mine were declining.

At one point, I grew curious about my opponent's strategy. The game used to have an option to chat with your opponent, which has since been removed. Back then, I took the opportunity to ask her why she was not buying any properties and simply replied that she was saving her money. I didn't understand the value of saving when I could buy assets at their market value, earning dividends when players landed on my properties.

Here's the revelation: I put into practice my opponent's strategy, and it took me some time to piece together the puzzle. This strategy allowed me to build up a significant cash reserve while my opponent was depleting cash by purchasing properties. When my opponent couldn't afford to buy properties at their market value anymore, they had to put these assets up for auction. With my increased cash reserves, I could easily outbid my opponent in auctions, buying assets well below their market value. This approach gave me a good margin of safety, as I continued to purchase high value properties while maintaining a strong cash position. Ultimately, this strategy gave me control over the game, tilting the odds in my favor and setting me up to win.

Adopting this strategy required a significant shift in mindset. It was about playing the long game, which meant forgoing immediate gratification for future gains. Each time I passed "Go" and collected my $200 salary, I resisted the urge to spend it impulsively. Instead, I watched the board, monitored my opponent's moves, and waited for opportunities.

The first few rounds were the hardest. Observing my opponent buying up properties while I sat on my cash seemed to go against common sense. However, as the game continued, the benefits of my new strategy became apparent. My opponent began to run out of cash, managing to pay rent or make necessary improvements. When properties went up for auction, my cash reserves allowed me to outbid my opponent easily.

They had to Mortgage off several of her properties for survival. With my substantial cash reserves, I was able to acquire these assets at a fraction of their market value. This was a turning point, as it significantly increased my property portfolio without compromising my financial stability.

As I continued to implement this strategy, the game began to shift in my favor. My opponent, who had spent all cash on buying properties, found unable to make further purchases. Times when my opponent landed on of my properties and couldn't afford to pay the rent force them to auction off or mortgage their properties which could no longer afford to maintain. With my substantial cash reserves, I was able to acquire these assets at a fraction of their market value.

This strategic taught me several valuable lessons about financial strategy and investment. The first was the importance of maintaining cash reserves for seizing opportunities and managing risks. In Monopoly, as in investing, cash is king. It provides the flexibility to act decisively and take advantage of situations that others might not be able to exploit due to financial constraints.

By holding onto cash, I was able to buy properties not just when they were available, but when they were cheap. This concept of buying low is a cornerstone of successful investing. In the real world, it translates to purchasing undervalued stocks or assets during market downturns. Just as I outbid my opponent in the game, savvy investors outbid others in the market by having the liquidity to buy when prices are low.

Another lesson was the value of patience and strategic planning. Instead of rushing into investments, sometimes it's better to wait for the right opportunity. This doesn't mean being passive; rather, it involves being actively engaged in watching and waiting for the right moment. In Monopoly, this meant holding back from buying properties until they were auctioned at a lower price. In real life, it means waiting for the right time to invest, such as during a market correction or when a particular asset is undervalued.

Furthermore, the experience underscored the importance of adaptability. My opponent's strategy forced me to rethink my approach and adapt my tactics. Flexibility is crucial in both games and real life. Markets are dynamic, and being able to adjust your strategy based on new information or changing circumstances can provide a significant advantage.

Acquiring assets below their market value not only offers potential for higher returns but also provides a cushion against market volatility. When you buy something at a discount, you create a margin of safety. This means that even if the market value drops further, your investment is still secure. This principle is widely endorsed by successful investors like Warren Buffett, who emphasize the importance of buying undervalued assets to minimize risk and maximize returns.

Moreover, maintaining a balance between assets and liquidity was another crucial takeaway. Owning high-value properties while keeping a significant amount of cash on hand meant I could continue to make strategic purchases and withstand any financial setbacks. This balance provided a solid foundation for long-term success, both in the game and in real-world investments.

As I refined my approach, I started to notice patterns and behaviors that I hadn't paid attention to before. For instance, the frequency with which certain properties were landed on, the likelihood of players going bankrupt if they overextended themselves, and the benefits of holding cash versus immediate property upgrades. These insights allowed me to fine-tune my strategy further.

My newfound approach not only helped me in Monopoly but also provided insights that I could apply to real-life financial decisions. It highlighted the importance of financial literacy and understanding the mechanisms behind investments. Monopoly became a simulation for real-world financial strategies, teaching me the importance of liquidity, strategic planning, and adaptability.

In Monopoly, just like in the real world, opportunities often arise from the financial distress of others. When my opponent was forced to auction off properties, I was able to capitalize on their difficult situation because I had prepared myself financially. This is akin to purchasing distressed assets in the stock market. Companies sometimes face financial difficulties that force them to sell assets or shares at a discount. Investors with cash reserves can take advantage of these situations to acquire valuable assets at a lower cost.

This experience also taught me the value of learning from others. My opponent's unconventional strategy was something I had never considered before. By observing and understanding my opponent's approach, I was able to improve my own tactics. In real life, being open to new ideas and learning from others can lead to significant personal and professional growth. It's important to stay curious, ask questions, and continuously seek knowledge.

Additionally, the game highlighted the power of concentrated investments. While the conventional wisdom often favors spreading investments across various properties, focusing on acquiring just two properties in one color set allowed me to leverage my position and significantly increase the rent I received. This strategy proved to be highly effective, illustrating that in certain scenarios, concentrated investments can yield higher returns. In real-life investing, concentrating on investments that you have thoroughly researched and are confident in can lead to greater financial success than diversifying widely. As Warren Buffett famously stated, having a few well-chosen businesses can provide a robust and diversified portfolio without the need for excessive spreading. Concentrated investments, when executed with due diligence, can change your financial trajectory profoundly.

As I continued to play and refine my strategies, I began to see Monopoly not just as a game, but as a sample of real-world economics and investment strategies. Each move, each decision, and each outcome offered a lesson in financial literacy. The game became a tool for practicing and honing skills that are directly applicable to real-life financial planning and investing.

For example, the concept of opportunity cost became clear to me through the game. By holding onto cash and waiting for the right moment to buy properties at auction, I was foregoing immediate returns in exchange for potentially higher future gains. In real life, opportunity cost is a critical concept in investing and decision-making. It involves considering the potential benefits you miss out on when choosing one investment over another. Understanding and evaluating opportunity costs can lead to more informed and strategic investment decisions.

Monopoly also taught me about the importance of long-term thinking. While short-term gains can be enticing, focusing on long-term goals and strategies often leads to more sustainable success. This principle applies to investing as well. Long-term investors who remain patient and stay the course are more likely to achieve their financial goals than those who chase short-term market fluctuations. Another important lesson from Monopoly is the impact of compounding. As I concentrated on properties and collected rent, my income increased, allowing me to make more strategic purchases and further expand my portfolio. This compounding effect is a powerful force in both the game and real-life investing.

CHAPTER TEN

RECLAIMING SUCCESS

"The stock market is filled with individuals who know the price of everything, but the value of nothing."

-Philip Fisher

A turnaround business often presents investors with an opportunity where a little creativity can go a long way. In many cases, screening for potential investments will lead us to discover businesses that seem to be priced attractively but, at first glance, reveal deteriorating financial statements. This might give the impression that these businesses are not good investment options. However, this is not always the case. As we've discussed earlier, finding a good business to invest in is not easy, but it's certainly not impossible. What investors often fail to realize is that there is significant value in looking beyond the surface when it comes to businesses that appear to be struggling.

When analyzing a business, it's crucial to remember that financial deterioration does not automatically spell failure. If a company is experiencing financial struggles, it's an opportunity for an investor to apply creativity and think outside the box. A business might have declining revenue, but the causes behind this decline can often offer valuable insight. If we dig deeper into the reasons for the downturn, we might uncover factors that others have overlooked. This is where we, as investors, have an advantage: our ability to see things that others may miss. We can look at the situation from a fresh perspective and, in doing so, we might uncover a gem that others dismiss too quickly.

It's not uncommon for a business to lose a significant client, resulting in a sharp drop in revenue. At first, this might look like a critical issue especially when you compare the lost revenue to the company's operating expenses. The survival of the business may appear to be in jeopardy. However, a critical question to ask is, "How long can the company survive given its financial strength?" A business might be facing challenges, but its financial resources might be strong enough to weather the storm. The key for investors is to assess how long the company can withstand the pressures it faces before its financial health deteriorates further.

Sometimes, a company's management may issue a comment about the loss of a major client, attempting to justify the decline. However, investors must take a more in-depth approach. How many quarters or even years will it take for the business to recover? What is the likelihood of the company regaining its lost revenue? The important thing to remember is that for every problem a business faces, there is a solution. While it may take time for the company to correct its course, this doesn't necessarily mean that the business is doomed. The problem that seems permanent at the moment may not be as permanent as it appears, and this is where the opportunity lies for investors.

When a company faces significant challenges, it can sometimes present a golden opportunity for investors. If we, as investors, are willing to take the time to dig deeper and understand the underlying causes of the business's struggles, we may find that the business is undervalued. The key is to be patient and wait for the business to prove itself, quarter by quarter or year by year. As long as the company is able to meet the expectations of its investors, there may be significant upside potential when the business turns around.

In theory, this approach sounds easy just wait for the business to meet expectations and take advantage of the steep discount in the meantime. In practice, however, investors need to dive deep into the problem and come up with a clear solution. We must carefully assess whether the company is on track to meet the expectations set by its investors. The solution to the problem may not always be the same for every business, but as long as the company shows steady progress, it is worth keeping an eye on. If a business can continue to meet investor expectations, even during difficult times, it can transform from a struggling company into a thriving one.

As investors, it's easy to be swept up in the excitement of a business turnaround. However, it's important to remain grounded and take a methodical approach to the situation. We should remember that businesses that experience a turnaround do so not because they simply rise from their struggles, but because they adapt, evolve, and ultimately prove their worth to investors. If we can understand and identify these patterns, we'll be in a position to make informed decisions and potentially benefit from the success of businesses that others have written off too soon.

The key is to be patient and take a long-term view. The short-term struggles of a business can often be the very thing that creates the best investment opportunities. If we wait for the business to turn its fortunes around, we can enter the market at a discounted price, confident that we are making an informed decision. Of course, this approach requires careful analysis and a deep understanding of the business's financials, market conditions, and management decisions. But when done correctly, it can yield substantial rewards.

Take, for example, the case of Ford Motor Company in the mid-2000s. Ford had experienced years of declining sales, high labor costs, and an overall loss of market share. In 2006, the company announced its plan for a major restructuring effort, which included selling off non-core assets, laying off employees, and reorganizing its product lineup. Despite these initial challenges, Ford's turnaround began to take shape with new leadership and a renewed focus on core competencies, particularly focusing on fuel-efficient vehicles during a time of rising oil prices. By 2011, Ford had returned to profitability and was able to avoid the government bailouts that its competitors, such as General Motors, required during the financial crisis. This example highlights how a company's ability to confront and overcome challenges can be a significant opportunity for investors who are willing to dig deeper into the story behind the numbers.

Reclaiming success

Similarly, Apple Inc. faced its own set of challenges in the late 1990s. After the departure of co-founder Steve Jobs and a string of poorly received products, the company was on the brink of bankruptcy. In 1997, Apple was losing money and struggling to compete with larger tech companies like Microsoft. However, after Jobs returned to the company and implemented a bold strategy of focusing on innovation, simplifying product offerings, and revamping the company's brand, Apple managed to turn things around. The launch of the iMac in 1998 was just the beginning of a transformation that would lead to some of the most successful products in consumer technology history. For investors, understanding the critical role of management, innovation, and the company's long-term vision during times of crisis is essential in identifying businesses that can weather storms and eventually come out stronger.

The core of investing in turnaround businesses lies in the ability to see beyond immediate problems and focus on the long-term potential. It's easy to be discouraged by declining revenue or increased operating expenses, but a deeper analysis can reveal important insights into a company's ability to recover. Consider the case of Netflix, which began as a DVD rental service and faced significant challenges in the early 2000s with rising competition and an evolving industry. In 2007, Netflix faced the risk of being left behind as online streaming began to emerge, and traditional cable companies were quickly innovating to offer similar services. However, Netflix made a bold decision to invest heavily in streaming technology and original content, which fundamentally shifted its business model. Today, Netflix is a dominant force in the entertainment industry, with millions of subscribers worldwide and a growing library of original programming. What was once seen as a declining business became one of the most profitable turnaround stories of the digital age.

Understanding why businesses falter and identifying the pathways that can lead to a successful recovery requires an investor to look at the underlying causes of a company's struggles. Revenue decline, for example, might result from the loss of a major client, but the key question is whether that revenue loss is a permanent issue or a temporary setback. If a company can survive long enough to either replace that lost revenue or reinvent its business model, it may be able to emerge stronger on the other side. Investors need to ask themselves how long the company can withstand these headwinds, whether the management has a clear plan for recovery, and how adaptable the company is to changing market conditions.

A prime example of a company that experienced a significant turnaround is Tesla. In the early 2010s, Tesla was on the brink of failure, struggling with production issues, limited cash flow, and skepticism about its future. Many analysts were quick to dismiss the company as a niche electric vehicle maker that couldn't compete with the traditional automakers. However, Tesla's CEO Elon Musk continued to innovate, invest in infrastructure, and scale production. The launch of the Model S in 2012 was a game-changer, and over the years, the company's growth accelerated. Today, Tesla is not only the leader in electric vehicles but also a major player in the renewable energy and technology sectors. The company's turnaround was the result of forward-thinking leadership, a relentless focus on technology and innovation, and a long-term vision that investor had to trust, even when the company was facing significant challenges.

In many cases, turnaround businesses might be overlooked by the broader market due to short-term concerns. This opens up opportunities for savvy investors to capitalize on undervalued stocks. The key is patience and a deep understanding of the business. If a company's fundamentals remain strong and it can weather temporary difficulties, it may offer substantial returns once the turnaround takes hold. However, this type of investment is not for the faint-hearted. It requires a level of creativity and confidence that allows investors to see opportunities where others might only see risks.

The process of identifying a turnaround business involves much more than just finding companies with declining financials or losses. It requires looking at the bigger picture and understanding the context behind these struggles. By focusing on the core aspects of the business, such as its revenue model, management decisions, product offerings, and the potential for growth, investors can uncover hidden gems. The turnaround story of Starbucks in the early 2000s serves as another perfect example. At a time when many thought Starbucks had peaked, the company's leadership recognized the need for change. Starbucks revitalized its product offerings, expanded its international presence, and embraced digital innovation, resulting in its return to growth and profitability.

While not every company will successfully navigate its way through difficult periods, history shows that many businesses that face adversity can emerge stronger and more profitable in the long run. For investors, the key to making successful turnaround investments lies in understanding that short-term setbacks can provide opportunities for long-term growth. The ability to identify these situations requires both analytical rigor and a creative approach to problem solving. By taking the time to research, evaluate, and understand the company's financial health, management, and strategy, investors can position themselves to reap the rewards of a well-timed turnaround investment.

In the end, the art of turnaround investing is about recognizing potential where others see failure. It involves digging deeper into the financials, understanding the underlying causes of the company's struggles, and assessing the management's ability to make necessary changes. While not every turnaround story has a happy ending, the ones that do can be some of the most rewarding investments, providing exceptional returns for investors who are willing to wait and take calculated risks. The best turnaround stories are those that demonstrate resilience, adaptability, and the ability to capitalize on opportunities, even in the face of adversity.

Index

1

10x return · 76

A

A watched pot never boils · 27
accountants · 25
accumulate · 24
accumulation · 73, 74
accurately · 55, 81, 84
Accuride Corporation · 60
achievements · 66, 69
achieving · 25, 30, 43, 50, 61, 66, 71, 87
acquire · 18, 19, 20, 46, 103, 106
acquiring · 16, 22, 38, 106
acquisition · 18, 19, 20
Afterpay · 19
AI-driven · 19
aligning · XII, XIII, 19, 21, 25, 39, 49, 65, 72, 93, 95
all-time high · 76, 77, 78, 79
ambition · 24, 66, 70
analogy · 17, 52
anxiety · 28, 76, 78
Apple Inc · 113
art · 22, 44, 50, 116
Asset-Based Valuation · 86, 87

assets · 17, 20, 38, 52, 53, 83, 84, 86, 95, 96, 102, 103, 104, 105, 106, 112
attractive · 46, 50, 51, 61, 64, 76
attractively · 109
avoiding · 26, 42, 75, 77, 79, 82
Axon Enterprise Inc. (AXON) · 67

B

bailouts · 112
balance sheets · 19, 94
bankruptcy · 57, 58, 59, 60, 61, 113
BC Aventura · 59
Bed Bath & Beyond · 59, 96
Behavioral · 21
Belk Department Store · 58
Benjamin Graham · 21
billion · XI, 18, 19, 20, 74, 83, 96
Block, Inc · 56
Blockbuster · 57
brand · 26, 42, 43, 45, 55, 67, 113
broader · 17, 20, 22, 26, 29, 30, 31, 33, 36, 52, 53, 54, 65, 72, 75, 91, 115
Buffett · XI, XII, 16, 18, 47

business economics · X, XII, 38, 56, 76, 77
buying back · 32, 98
buys and sells · 27

C

calculated · 27, 116
calculated risks · 27, 116
capital · X, XII, 15, 16, 25, 31, 35, 36, 37, 38, 44, 48, 49, 53, 56, 57, 58, 64, 65, 78, 85, 95, 97
capitalize · 20, 23, 39, 53, 67, 73, 75, 106, 115, 116
CareMax · 59
cash · 18, 19, 20, 37, 44, 56, 57, 65, 73, 74, 75, 76, 85, 96, 97, 98, 101, 102, 103, 104, 105, 106, 107, 114
cash flow · 44, 56, 57, 65, 97, 98, 114
cash reserves · 19, 20, 37, 73, 74, 75, 97, 101, 102, 103, 104, 106
CEOs · 69
challenges · XII, XIII, 23, 24, 45, 46, 49, 50, 51, 58, 59, 60, 61, 65, 67, 68, 84, 90, 91, 95, 110, 111, 112, 113, 115
challenging · 25, 65, 83
Charlie Munger · XII, 21
charts · IX, 25
Chipotle Mexican Grill, Inc. · 69
clear path · 81

cohesive · 26
Colicity Inc · 61
communication · 20, 24, 68
companies · XI, XII, 15, 17, 18, 19, 20, 29, 30, 33, 35, 36, 37, 41, 42, 43, 44, 46, 47, 49, 50, 52, 53, 57, 63, 64, 68, 70, 71, 75, 85, 86, 94, 95, 113, 115
Comparable Company Analysis · 85, 87
competence · 24, 42, 51, 61
competitive · 20, 22, 25, 26, 33, 38, 42, 43, 45, 50, 68, 82, 83, 90, 93, 94
complicated · 18, 48
compounding · XI, 21, 24, 37, 79, 108
comprehensive · XII, 22, 38, 56, 81, 86, 89, 91
concentrating · 17, 106
conditions · 24, 76, 83, 86, 90, 112, 114
confidence · 23, 32, 36, 51, 67, 69, 71, 79, 84, 115
confident · 65, 67, 87, 95, 107, 112
consumers · 19
conviction · 22, 25, 26, 27, 66, 90
Conviction · 25, 26
Core Scientific Inc · 60
Country Fresh · 58
crucial · XI, 16, 18, 20, 26, 30, 31, 34, 44, 52, 56, 63, 66, 67, 68, 74, 78, 79, 81, 82, 89, 91, 93, 104, 105, 109

culture · 22, 63, 68, 69
currency · 18, 19
cyclical · 23, 45, 52, 74

D

damage · 24
debt · 15, 18, 19, 20, 35, 44, 56, 57, 58, 59, 60, 64, 95, 96, 97, 98
decisions · X, XI, XII, 21, 22, 29, 30, 31, 32, 33, 38, 43, 47, 49, 56, 57, 63, 64, 65, 66, 67, 70, 71, 75, 76, 77, 78, 79, 86, 87, 90, 93, 95, 96, 97, 98, 99, 105, 107, 112, 115
demand · 16, 25, 34, 36, 52, 60, 65, 73, 89, 92
deterioration · 96, 109
develop · 25, 29, 86
diligence · 26, 71, 83, 107
dimension · 27
dip in its stock price · 23
disciplined · XI, 17, 22, 24, 30, 45, 47, 74, 87
discount · 46, 85, 105, 106, 111
discounted · 23, 85, 112
Discounted Cash Flow (DCF) · 84
discounted price · 23
discounts · 52, 73
disposable income · 79
distribution · 42, 73, 74
dividends · 20, 41, 44, 78, 79, 97, 98, 99, 102

downturns · 21, 24, 26, 42, 44, 47, 81, 90, 95, 104
dynamics · 16, 22, 28, 31, 32, 36, 39, 41, 43, 47, 53, 73, 74, 82

E

earnings · 23, 38, 42, 44, 45, 55, 56, 67, 70, 75
earnings miss · 23, 75
economic · 21, 24, 42, 44, 51, 75, 76, 77, 90, 95
economic indicators · 21
edge · 19, 20, 26, 31, 42, 43, 45, 46, 54, 83, 96
Elon Musk · 70, 114
emotional reactions · 26, 75
emphasized · 47, 81
emphasizes · XI, XII, 15, 30, 42, 71
Enphase Energy, · 69, 71
equity · 19, 20, 37, 44, 95, 98
essentials · 17
Etsy Inc · 68
evaluating · 24, 25, 27, 42, 56, 57, 63, 69, 70, 71, 82, 84, 92, 95, 107
executives · 32, 69, 70
expectations · 17, 64, 111
Expectations · 61
Exxon Mobil Corporation · 18

F

factors · 21, 22, 23, 25, 26, 31, 34, 43, 51, 56, 61, 69, 71, 78, 83, 87, 110
father of value investing · 21
fear and greed · 21
fears · 78
finance · 18, 21, 35, 95
financial · X, XII, XIII, 15, 18, 19, 20, 25, 30, 31, 33, 34, 39, 41, 43, 44, 49, 57, 58, 59, 60, 61, 63, 64, 65, 66, 70, 73, 79, 83, 84, 85, 86, 89, 94, 95, 96, 98, 99, 103, 104, 105, 106, 107, 109, 110, 112, 116
financial statements · 25, 43, 63, 64, 70, 84, 89, 96, 109
financials · 22, 45, 50, 51, 64, 65, 81, 99, 112, 115, 116
flexibility · 18, 44, 104
fluctuate · 21
fluctuation · 17
fluctuations · 16, 17, 26, 29
focus · XII, 17, 21, 27, 29, 42, 45, 46, 49, 53, 65, 66, 67, 74, 75, 87, 92, 112, 113, 115
footprint · 18, 20
form of payment · 19
foundation · X, XIII, 22, 25, 50, 51, 65, 76, 77, 105
framework · 22, 27, 71
Free float · 33
fundamental · 15, 16, 23, 70, 73, 81, 84, 87, 89, 90, 97
fundamentals · XI, 16, 24, 25, 26, 39, 42, 53, 54, 74, 75, 76, 79, 83, 115
future · IX, XII, XIII, 22, 25, 36, 37, 39, 48, 49, 52, 64, 65, 67, 69, 72, 74, 77, 78, 83, 85, 90, 93, 94, 95, 98, 103, 107, 114

G

gaining · 20
General Motors · 112
Glassdoor · 68
goals · XIII, 17, 21, 25, 30, 36, 38, 41, 49, 50, 64, 65, 66, 70, 71, 72, 78, 79, 96, 107
gross profit margins · 93
grow a business · 64
growth · XIII, 15, 16, 17, 18, 19, 21, 22, 24, 25, 27, 29, 31, 32, 33, 35, 36, 37, 38, 39, 41, 44, 45, 48, 52, 53, 55, 56, 65, 67, 68, 69, 71, 72, 75, 78, 79, 82, 83, 85, 87, 90, 91, 92, 93, 94, 95, 97, 98, 106, 114, 115, 116
growth prospects · 15, 48, 75, 82, 83, 85

H

Healthcare Service Group, Inc · 98
Hewlett Packard Enterprise · 19

hidden gem · 26
highlights · 15, 19, 30, 66, 70, 92, 93, 94, 96, 112
high-profile · 26
history · 21, 24, 41, 42, 69, 113, 115
hobby · 77
homework · 23
Howard Marks · 30

I

identifying · 22, 24, 25, 46, 50, 71, 87, 113, 114, 115
impact · 37, 55, 68, 70, 71, 72, 76, 108
impatience · 27
implications · 28, 31
improvement · XII, 64
industry · 22, 24, 25, 43, 45, 46, 50, 53, 54, 66, 68, 69, 70, 82, 83, 84, 85, 90, 91, 95, 113, 114
influence · 21, 22, 31, 35, 63, 78, 97
influences · 22, 41, 74, 75
inherently · 23, 37, 49, 82
Initial Public Offering · 15, 16
insiders · 31, 32, 33, 34, 35
insights · 21, 24, 26, 27, 35, 43, 63, 64, 67, 68, 69, 71, 86, 92, 93, 105, 113
intellectual property · 26
intervention · 29

intrinsic · 17, 21, 36, 37, 45, 77, 78, 79, 81, 82, 83, 84, 85, 87
Intrum · 60
intuition · 22, 25, 41, 84
Investing · XIII, 15, 17, 24, 25, 42, 47, 49, 51, 53, 66, 74, 75, 82, 101
investment · IX, X, XI, XII, 17, 21, 22, 23, 24, 25, 26, 29, 30, 33, 39, 41, 45, 47, 50, 57, 61, 63, 65, 70, 71, 74, 75, 76, 77, 78, 79, 81, 82, 83, 84, 86, 87, 90, 91, 92, 96, 101, 104, 105, 107, 109, 112, 115, 116
investment strategies · 22, 63, 74, 107
investors · X, 15, 17, 20, 21, 22, 23, 25, 26, 27, 28, 29, 30, 31, 32, 33, 34, 35, 36, 37, 39, 41, 42, 43, 44, 45, 46, 47, 49, 52, 53, 54, 55, 56, 57, 63, 64, 65, 66, 67, 69, 70, 71, 73, 74, 75, 76, 77, 78, 79, 81, 82, 84, 85, 86, 87, 89, 90, 91, 93, 94, 95, 96, 97, 98, 99, 104, 105, 107, 109, 110, 111, 112, 113, 115, 116
IPO · 15, 16, 32, 70
irrational · XI, 16, 21, 73
irrationality · 17

J

John Bogle · 21
journey · IX, XIII, 27, 49, 56, 77

Juniper Networks · 19

Losses · 17

K

key · 17, 30, 38, 44, 47, 48, 50, 54, 56, 61, 70, 74, 79, 83, 84, 85, 87, 110, 111, 112, 114, 115, 116

L

landscape · 22, 25, 29, 41, 43, 82, 93
leadership · 24, 39, 42, 43, 63, 64, 67, 68, 69, 70, 71, 91, 112, 115
leading · 19, 22, 38, 46, 47, 58, 65, 74, 90, 95
lesson · 17, 27, 104, 107, 108
leverage · 18, 19, 43, 106
liquidate · 34, 77
liquidity · 32, 33, 35, 95, 104, 105, 106
long term · 20, 24, 26, 34, 35, 37, 38, 41, 42, 45, 49, 50, 61, 65
long-term · XI, XIII, 17, 18, 19, 20, 21, 22, 23, 24, 25, 26, 28, 29, 30, 32, 33, 36, 37, 38, 39, 49, 51, 53, 57, 64, 65, 66, 67, 68, 71, 75, 76, 77, 78, 79, 90, 92, 95, 96, 98, 99, 105, 107, 112, 113, 115, 116
long-Term · 16

M

management · IX, 22, 23, 24, 26, 27, 30, 33, 34, 36, 38, 43, 44, 45, 51, 56, 57, 63, 64, 65, 66, 67, 68, 69, 70, 71, 72, 76, 77, 91, 93, 95, 96, 97, 98, 99, 110, 112, 113, 114, 115, 116
management team · 22, 24, 63, 67, 69, 71
managing · 21, 30, 65, 103, 104
manipulation · 32, 34
mark-down · 73, 74
market · IX, X, XI, XII, XIII, 16, 17, 18, 19, 20, 21, 22, 23, 25, 26, 27, 28, 29, 30, 31, 32, 33, 34, 36, 38, 39, 41, 42, 43, 45, 46, 47, 48, 51, 52, 53, 54, 55, 56, 57, 59, 61, 65, 66, 73, 74, 75, 76, 77, 78, 79, 81, 83, 84, 85, 86, 87, 89, 90, 91, 92, 93, 94, 95, 102, 103, 104, 105, 108, 112, 114, 115
Market cycles · 73
market drop · 28
market fluctuations · XI, 23, 34, 66, 75, 77
Market volatility · 21
mark-up · 73, 74
media hype · 78
Mediocre · 66
mediocrity · 83
metaphorical · 27

mid-cap · 68, 74, 75
Midland · 18
misconceptions · 16
model · XI, 22, 43, 45, 51, 54, 56, 66, 83, 84, 85, 90, 91, 92, 113, 114, 115
monitor · IX, 17
Monopoly · 101, 104, 105, 106, 107, 108
Monster Beverage Corporation · 55
monthly · 29

N

navigate · X, 24, 30, 50, 75, 79, 91, 95, 115
Netflix · 54, 57, 113
news · XI, 23, 28, 75, 76
niche · 53, 55, 67, 68, 114
Nordic Aviation Group · 59
Northvolt · 59
nuances · 63, 70, 90
numbers · 22, 26, 27, 63, 64, 65, 112

O

observer effect · 27, 28, 29
operating margins · 93
operational efficiency · 38, 43, 91, 94
opportunities · XIII, 18, 20, 22, 23, 24, 25, 27, 35, 36, 39, 41, 42, 44, 46, 48, 52, 53, 67, 71, 73, 74, 75, 87, 94, 95, 103, 104, 106, 112, 115, 116
opportunity · XII, 23, 26, 27, 48, 73, 75, 84, 90, 99, 102, 104, 107, 109, 111, 112
opportunity to buy · 23
optimistic · 73, 74
organization · 22, 65
over-monitoring · 28
ownership · 31, 32, 33, 35, 36, 39, 101
owning a piece · 16

P

panic · 26, 34, 47
panic selling · 26, 34
Paper Source · 58
Party City · 58
patience · XI, XIII, 18, 21, 23, 24, 27, 29, 49, 50, 53, 65, 87, 104, 115
peak · 77
pension funds · X, 33, 34
pension funds, hedge funds, and mutual funds · 33
Permian Basins · 18
perspective · 17, 20, 21, 22, 24, 25, 29, 68, 79, 85, 110
pessimistic · 73, 75
Peter Lynch · 18, 30, 94
physics and psychology · 28
Pier 1 Imports · 57
Pioneer · 18

111

Planet Fitness, Inc · 68
plans · 19, 26, 67, 93
point · 23, 27, 48, 73, 90, 99, 102, 103
political events · 21
popularity · 26
portfolio · 20, 25, 27, 28, 29, 46, 47, 48, 49, 50, 77, 79, 103, 107, 108
position · IX, 20, 23, 38, 43, 48, 64, 75, 76, 77, 78, 102, 106, 112, 116
power · XI, XIII, 18, 29, 101, 106
power of investing · 29
powerful · 22, 25, 27, 38, 43, 64, 66, 108
Precedent Transactions Analysis · 86
price · XI, 16, 17, 18, 23, 27, 31, 32, 33, 34, 35, 36, 37, 38, 45, 46, 47, 48, 74, 75, 76, 77, 79, 81, 82, 104, 109, 112
Price to Book (P/B) · 82
Price to Earnings (P/E) · 82, 85
Price to Free Cash Flow · 82
Price to Sales (P/S) · 82, 85
principle · XII, 16, 28, 42, 81, 85, 105, 107
principles · 16, 18, 22, 30, 45, 50, 71
proactive · 24, 95
problem · XI, 23, 56, 110, 111, 116
problems · 23, 24, 90, 113

products · 22, 26, 43, 45, 51, 60, 61, 76, 78, 89, 92, 93, 113
profit margins · 44, 85, 91, 93
profitability · 17, 32, 33, 38, 42, 44, 53, 54, 59, 60, 64, 65, 83, 91, 93, 94, 112, 115
projections · 64
promising · 26, 66, 77, 93
properties · 52, 86, 101, 102, 103, 104, 105, 106, 107, 108
prospects · 24, 25, 26, 33, 36, 49, 65, 75, 76, 78, 79, 83, 90, 93
psychological · 21, 22
Psychologically · 28
purchase · 15, 16, 19, 20, 73, 76, 77, 102
puzzle · 17, 18, 102

Q

qualitative · 22, 24, 25, 26, 27, 43, 69, 82, 87
qualitative analysis · 22, 24
quantitative · 22, 25, 26, 27, 43, 65, 82, 87
Quantitative analysis · 64
quantum mechanics · 28
quarterly · 75
questions · 25, 64, 67, 106

R

ratios · 25, 95, 97
realistic · 17, 84
real-world · 18, 86, 105, 106, 107
recovery · 28, 69, 90, 114
research · IX, 17, 22, 25, 26, 41, 47, 56, 57, 65, 67, 75, 78, 93, 116
researched · 46, 77, 79, 107
resilience · 24, 25, 27, 51, 91, 92, 95, 116
resilient · 25, 50, 57
responsibilities · 65
restricted · 31, 32, 33, 34
retail · X, 17, 33, 35, 39, 45, 53, 65, 96, 97, 99
retail investors · 33, 35, 39, 53, 97, 99
revenue · 44, 45, 46, 51, 55, 56, 57, 60, 61, 63, 65, 83, 84, 89, 90, 91, 92, 93, 94, 109, 110, 113, 114, 115
rewards · 17, 24, 42, 49, 57, 112, 116
risk factors · 56
risk management · 30
Risk Management · 57
risks · 24, 25, 30, 38, 51, 56, 57, 61, 69, 71, 85, 87, 96, 104, 115
Rite Aid · 59
robust · 20, 27, 39, 42, 50, 69, 71, 76, 83, 90, 95, 107

robust strategy · 27

S

Salesforce · 19, 20
Sally's Restaurant & Grill · 60
savings · 79, 95
science · 22, 28, 44, 50
secret formula · 22, 82
sector · 19, 22, 42, 45, 49, 74
seize · 24, 27, 44, 73, 95
sell · 20, 28, 32, 33, 35, 74, 75, 77, 78, 106
selloffs · 23, 34
sentiment · 16, 17, 21, 27, 34, 74
share repurchase · 98
shareholders · 16, 18, 19, 20, 31, 35, 36, 37, 38, 44, 66, 76, 97, 99
Shares outstanding · 31
short-term · 21, 23, 24, 26, 28, 32, 37, 57, 67, 75, 78, 90, 107, 108, 112, 115, 116
short-term market fluctuations · 21, 108
sidelines · 27
significantly · 19, 21, 33, 34, 36, 37, 48, 57, 71, 76, 82, 92, 102, 103, 106
simple idea · 27
Slack · 19, 20
small cap and mid cap · 71
source · 20, 97
speculation · 16, 75, 93

Spirit Airlines · 59
spreadsheets · 25
Square's · 19
stages · 27, 55, 73
stake · 23, 35, 37
stakeholders · 32, 92
stock deal · 19
stock market · IX, X, XII, 16, 17, 20, 21, 28, 30, 31, 41, 49, 50, 52, 53, 57, 75, 78, 79, 81, 106, 109
stock price · 18, 32, 48
stock splits · 32
stock value · 18
stocks · IX, 15, 16, 20, 21, 22, 27, 33, 39, 41, 42, 46, 47, 50, 51, 53, 54, 61, 66, 73, 79, 87, 94, 104, 115
strategic · 18, 19, 20, 26, 29, 37, 38, 43, 51, 54, 55, 63, 64, 65, 67, 70, 86, 91, 92, 95, 102, 104, 105, 106, 107, 108
strategic acquisitions · 18
strategies · 4, X, 38, 61, 66, 67, 68, 94, 95, 106, 107
strategy · X, XI, XIII, 17, 19, 22, 28, 29, 36, 37, 39, 41, 47, 53, 56, 64, 78, 79, 87, 91, 101, 102, 103, 104, 105, 106, 113, 116
strength · 18, 26, 44, 65, 76, 110
strengths and weaknesses lie · 92
struggling · 64, 109, 111, 113, 114

Studying · 21
success · XIII, 17, 18, 20, 21, 22, 25, 30, 32, 33, 39, 41, 42, 43, 50, 51, 52, 55, 57, 61, 63, 64, 66, 67, 68, 70, 71, 75, 77, 78, 89, 90, 91, 93, 94, 96, 97, 98, 99, 105, 107, 112
successful investor · 16
suggesting · 30
supply · 16, 34, 58, 59, 73
sustainable · 16, 25, 32, 42, 50, 57, 69, 71, 72, 92, 95, 107

T

Taco Bell's · 69
tangible · 64, 83, 84, 86
temporary · XI, 23, 25, 26, 46, 77, 90, 114, 115
temporary problems · 23
Temporary setbacks · 23, 90
Tesla · 49, 53, 70, 114
TGIF · 60
The College of Saint Rose · 60
thesis · 23, 26, 27, 47, 50, 77, 79
time · IX, XI, XII, 15, 16, 24, 27, 28, 29, 31, 32, 36, 41, 43, 46, 47, 48, 49, 50, 53, 55, 56, 57, 65, 66, 71, 74, 76, 77, 78, 79, 85, 86, 91, 93, 101, 102, 103, 104, 110, 111, 112, 115, 116
track record · 24, 69
track records · 67, 71

trading · IX, X, 16, 26, 34, 36, 48, 74, 77, 82
traditional · XII, 26, 46, 53, 54, 55, 58, 72, 113, 114
transaction · 19, 20
transactions · 16, 34, 86
transparent · 24, 68, 70
true · 21, 25, 28, 50, 52, 64, 75, 83, 84, 87
true value · 21
trust · 24, 26, 27, 29, 43, 115
Tuesday Morning Corporation · 60

U

uncertainty · 23, 26
underlying · 16, 26, 65, 73, 74, 75, 77, 83, 111, 114, 116
understanding · X, XIII, 15, 22, 23, 24, 25, 26, 29, 30, 34, 35, 36, 38, 41, 43, 49, 51, 52, 53, 56, 57, 61, 65, 66, 70, 73, 75, 77, 78, 81, 83, 84, 85, 86, 87, 94, 96, 97, 98, 105, 106, 112, 113, 115, 116
undervalued · 17, 22, 39, 45, 52, 53, 54, 55, 83, 85, 87, 104, 105, 111, 115
unlock · 22
unrestricted · 31, 32, 33, 34
upside · 52, 111

V

validates · 27, 91, 92
valuation methods · 86
valuations · 16, 19, 20, 46, 50, 55, 82, 83, 86
value · 16, 17, 18, 21, 22, 24, 25, 26, 29, 32, 33, 35, 36, 37, 38, 43, 44, 45, 48, 49, 52, 54, 66, 67, 71, 73, 74, 75, 76, 77, 78, 79, 81, 82, 83, 84, 85, 86, 87, 92, 97, 98, 102, 103, 104, 105, 106, 109
Visa, Inc · 93, 94
vision · 22, 24, 26, 43, 64, 65, 66, 67, 68, 70, 113, 115
visionary · 66, 70
volatility · XIII, 21, 23, 26, 29, 32, 33, 34, 42, 46, 79, 87, 105

W

Warren Buffett · XI, 15, 17, 21, 42, 47, 77, 89, 105, 107
wealth · X, XI, XII, XIII, 27, 36, 53, 66
worth · XI, XII, 17, 35, 37, 49, 53, 57, 69, 75, 83, 94, 95, 96, 111

Y

year · XI, XIII, 29, 56, 64, 91, 93, 97, 98, 111

yield · 36, 82, 98, 106, 112

Thank you for reading!

If you enjoyed this book, please consider leaving a review on the website where you purchased it. Your feedback is greatly appreciated and it helps other readers discover new books.

www.ingramcontent.com/pod-product-compliance
Lightning Source LLC
Chambersburg PA
CBHW031425210526
45464CB00005B/2059